EAST BAY OUT

An unauthorized guide to hiking, camping, swimming, and fishing in the East Bay Regional Parks

MALCOLM MARGOLIN

illustrations
NANCY CURRY

Many people helped make this book, and I'm especially grateful to:

Rina, wife, collaborator, and map designer whose creativity shows throughout the book;

Larry diStasi, friend, editor, and proofreader, ear when I needed an ear, voice when I was looking for a voice;

Hal Hershey who shared his knowledge, his strength and his friendship;

Monte Monteagle, amateur historian and head of the East Bay Regional Park District's news bureau, who let me draw freely from his research, his files, and his enthusiasm;

Kent Watson, Dave Hupp, Dick Raymond, Mary Jefferds, Strawdog, Clifford Burke, Scott Swanton, Pete Wickware, Ron Russo, and Tim Gordon who helped in many important ways;

And finally my mother, Rose L. Margolin, to whom I affectionately dedicate this book.

Calligraphy by Barbara Bash

Published by Heyday Books
Box 9145
Berkeley, California 94709

Contents

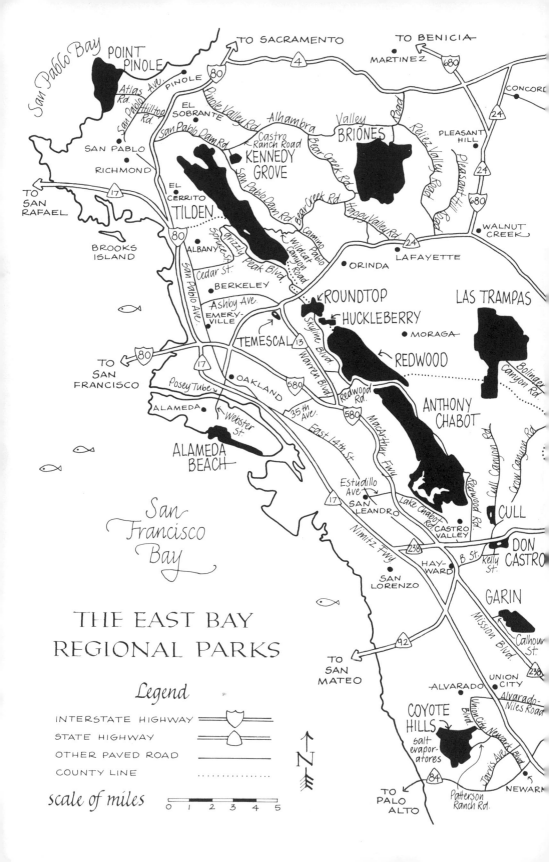

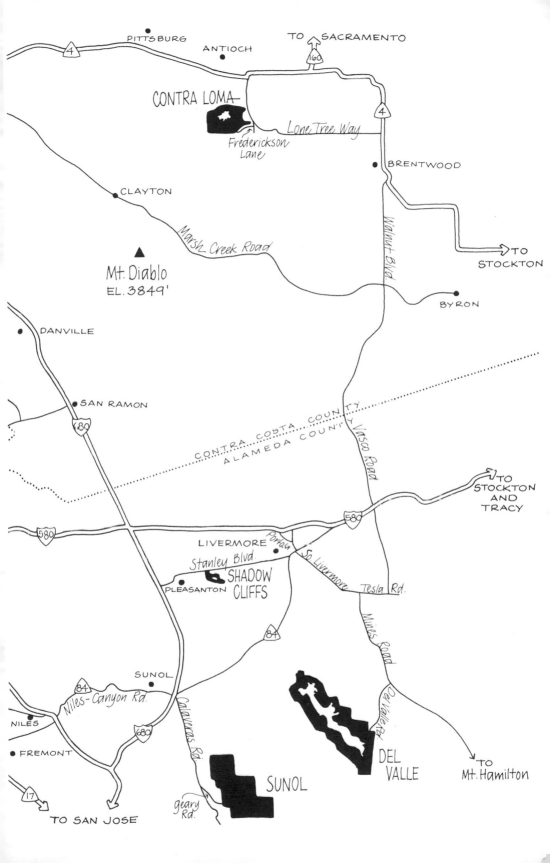

Hills

For those of us living in the flatlands of the East Bay, the hills that rise up behind us are like a theatrical backdrop. Long ago when tiny bands of Costanoan Indians were collecting shellfish from the Bay, or when the Spanish first settled here on their sprawling *ranchos,* this backdrop of green hills was appropriate to the pastoral dramas being played on the broad stage of the flatlands.

But cities grew up along the shores of the Bay. They became bigger, denser, more exciting, and more frantic, until today most of us are unwilling actors in an immensely complicated play we can't begin to understand. The magnificent backdrop of the hills seems sadly out of place against our modern cities. Indeed there are real estate developers who would like nothing better than to decorate it with houses and roads —— a scenery more in line with the current performance.

Fortunately, the real estate developers have not succeeded. And on warm summer mornings, on clear winter days, on spring weekends, some of us escape from the stage, shake off our roles, tell the crazy producers and directors that we've had it up to here; and we climb into that backdrop, into the folds and ridges of the scenic curtain, through its meadows and its forests, into the land of the Costanoans, high up into the hills, where we find.....

Briones

Briones Regional Park is a 3,000 acre semi-wilderness area that lies between
Lafayette and Martinez. It is an area of high bucking hills, broad valleys, creeks,
meadows, ponds, waterfalls, and forests. You cannot drive your car past the two
entrance gates, so this is a park primarily for hikers. And the hiking is splendid.
The hills have a glorious, windy, high-country feeling to them —— the sort of
wild feeling that makes you want to break loose and run like a joyous crazy down
the rippling meadows. The valleys (Abrigo, Homestead, Willow Flat, and Bear
Creek) are wide, motherly valleys that gurgle with springs and song birds. People
stop to picnic, often in the shade of a massive valley oak, and even those who have
never so much as planted a radish seed begin to daydream about owning a farm
in a place "just like this." Cattle graze on the meadows, deer browse at the edges
of the woods, hawks play with the breezes overhead, and an occasional hiker wan-
ders through this huge park, lost in wonderment at it all.

Briones is a park where —— especially on overcast days —— you are likely to
see more deer than hikers. Deer are everywhere. They push their long, gentle faces
into the cool grass of the meadows. They munch acorns thoughtfully at the edges
of the forests. They cluster together in small clearings as if posing for a family por-
trait. Keep a sharp eye out, and sticking out of the brush you will probably see
those erect ears, tensed bodies, frozen faces, and big unblinking eyes that watch
your every move. Maintain a polite distance, and they continue to stare at you.
Edge closer and they trot gracefully away. But move toward them suddenly and
they boing-boing-boing away into the nearest thicket as if on pogo sticks.

While deer are always shy and demure, the cattle here seem at first to be almost
malevolent —— especially when a big herd of them is blocking your path. This
puts the urban hiker into a dilemma. Should he act the role of a coward and give
the cattle wide berth? Or should he plunge right through them, preparing to ex-
ecute a half-veronica in the style of Juan Belmonte?

If you find yourself with this problem, be assured there is nothing to worry about.
The brown cattle with the white faces are Herefords, and they are very docile. The

black cattle are Angus. While Angus bulls are supposed to be testy, the young steers and heifers at Briones are far from dangerous. So walk resolutely toward them, and the herd of baleful looking beasts will obligingly scatter before you.

But what are cattle doing in this semi-wilderness park in the first place? Don't they trample the wildflowers, compete with the deer, and totally upset the balance of nature? Wouldn't Briones be much better off without them?

The truth is that rather than being intruders, cattle are actually the creators of the East Bay grassland environment. When the Spanish first settled here 150 years ago, the meadowlands of this area were covered with perennial grasses —— the so-called "bunch grasses," with their long, tough roots and their ability to survive the summer's heat. The Spanish lost no time in introducing cattle. Tangled in the hair of the cattle were the seeds of the European grasses —— grasses that die back each summer and grow again from seed in the fall, grasses that eventually were to take over the East Bay meadowlands almost completely.

By changing the grasslands of the East Bay, cattle may have created a permanent niche for themselves here, especially in the drier, inland areas like Briones. Without their grazing, the annual grasses would grow waist-high, die back in the summer, and become a major fire hazard. Also, cattle are valuable for browsing on brush which might otherwise invade the fields of comparatively weak-rooted annual grasses.

Except for the change of grasses, though, Briones seems to be quite unspoiled. I doubt if the mosaic of dense forests and open meadows has changed much since 1829 when Felipe Briones, a retired Spanish soldier, fell in love with a waterfall here and decided to settle upon the land. For the next decade he lived peacefully, supporting his family of eighteen. But in 1839 a band of Indians stole horses from his neighbor, Ygnacio Martinez. Felipe Briones, the ex-soldier, was called upon to help recover the horses. In the battle which followed he was struck by an arrow and killed. After his death his widow, Dona Maria Manuela Valencia de Briones, received title to 13,353 acres (nearly 25 square miles), of which Briones Regional Park covers only a small part. Most of the rest of this once vast *rancho* has been acquired by the East Bay Municipal Utility District as part of the San Pablo Reservoir watershed.

Those of us who know Briones well feel that this is one of the most exciting places in the East Bay. It is a wild park with lots of space. Hikers along Briones Crest enjoy splendid views of the Bay, Mount Diablo, and (on clear days) the

Sierras in the distance. But they are probably totally unaware of other hikers who are exploring the shady forested canyons, the creeks, ponds, and waterfalls.

I visit Briones often, but my own favorite time of year is fall when this big park first shakes off its summer sleep. As the days get cooler and shorter, certain trees (most notably the big-leaf maples) turn fall colors. The thick forests of Briones become dappled with yellows, browns, and russets. Leaves of the climbing grape vines shoot bold touches of red throughout the trees. Hark ye, hark ye, all you displaced New Englanders: there is a rich and colorful autumn to be found in the woodlands of Briones.

The second great autumn change in Briones comes with the first rains. All summer the meadows lay dry and golden, a slumbering giant. With the first rains the giant awakens. A million, billion grass seeds burst open, and waves of green wash over the golden hills.

Newts are among the first to celebrate. After the first heavy rains thousands and thousands of newts (or salamanders, as they're sometimes called) appear throughout Briones as if by spontaneous generation. On cool, rainy fall days it's hard to find a square yard of grassland or forest that doesn't have its own resident newt. They have the same shape as lizards, but totally different personalities. Lizards are sunshine creatures, light and fast. Newts, on the other hand, are creatures of moist dank places. They are stiff and sluggish, with cold rubbery skin. They act as if they had just crawled out of the refrigerator and haven't quite warmed up yet. You can easily pick one up, handle it, and put it down. Rub its back lightly and it will go into a "defensive position." It is a minor miracle that such a sluggish creature ever catches anything to eat.

By late autumn the ponds and lagoons in the hills fill once again with water. Freshwater ponds are rare in the Bay Area, so be sure to enjoy them while you're here. Peer into one of these ponds and you will see schools of tiny fish shimmering this way and that. Frogs croak at each other with unabashed machismo. Freshwater snails meticulously explore the newly submerged grasses.

The creeks of Briones also begin to flow again. In early fall there are only tenuous splatterings and murmurings, but by late winter the creeks become boisterous and high spirited. Waterfalls splash and dash happily along Cascade Creek, ferns spill over the banks, and in the dark canyons drops of water glisten like jewels in the green micro-worlds of moss.

By Christmas time the water has won its battle against the summer drought. Elsewhere snow may be falling and icicles forming, but in the East Bay we have every reason to be celebrating the annual miracle of a green Christmas.

By early spring the grasses become tall and loose, waving and rippling sensuously in the meadows. Thousands of sluggish newts now make their way to the

10

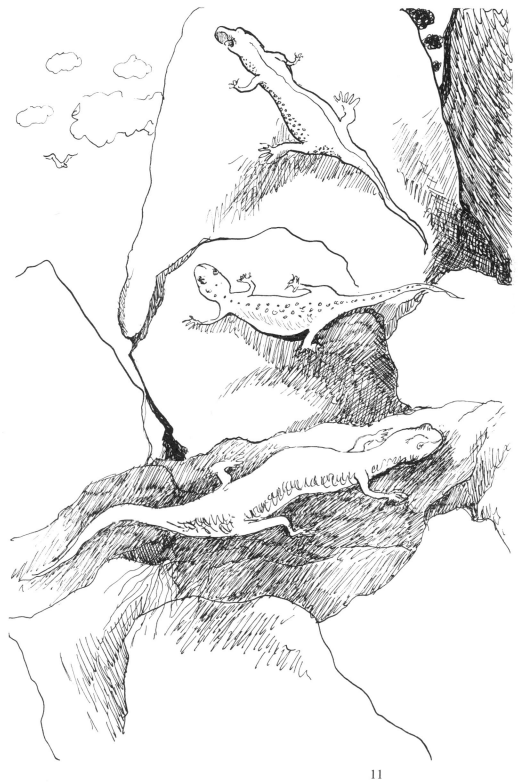

BRIONES
3,057 acres

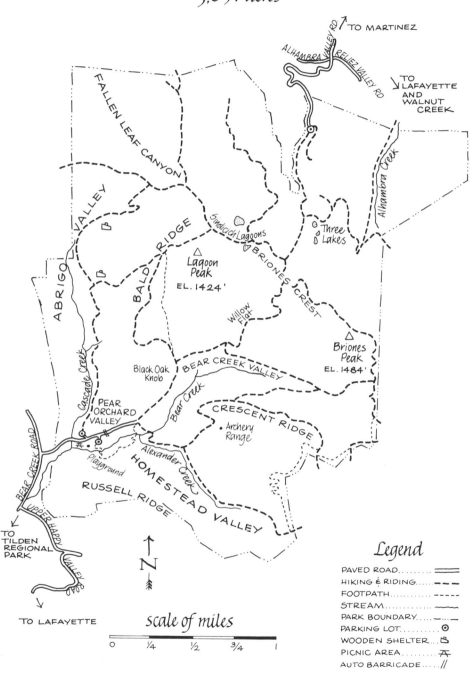

TO MARTINEZ

ALHAMBRA VALLEY RD

RELIEZ VALLEY RD

TO LAFAYETTE AND WALNUT CREEK

FALLEN LEAF CANYON

Alhambra Creek

ABRIGO VALLEY

BALD RIDGE

Smolich Lagoons

Three Lakes

Lagoon Peak
EL. 1424'

BRIONES CREST

Willow Flat

Cascade Creek

Black Oak Knob

Briones Peak
EL. 1484'

BEAR CREEK VALLEY

Bear Creek

PEAR ORCHARD VALLEY

CRESCENT RIDGE

Archery Range

Playground

Alexander Creek

BEAR CREEK ROAD

HOMESTEAD VALLEY

RUSSELL RIDGE

UPPER HAPPY VALLEY ROAD

TO TILDEN REGIONAL PARK

TO LAFAYETTE

N

scale of miles

0   ¼   ½   ¾   1

Legend

PAVED ROAD	═══
HIKING & RIDING	▬ ▬ ▬
FOOTPATH	‑ ‑ ‑ ‑
STREAM	∼∼
PARK BOUNDARY	▬ ‑ ▬ ‑
PARKING LOT	⊙
WOODEN SHELTER	⌂
PICNIC AREA	⊼
AUTO BARRICADE	//

ponds for their springtime mating orgy. In the water they take on a new, romantic identity. They tuck their legs in against their bodies, and with a few strong undulations of the tail they propel themselves through the water as quickly and effortlessly as fish. By late March the newts disappear entirely, the meadows are dotted with wildflowers and with cows, the grass bolts to seed, and the land prepares itself once again for the hot dry summer.

To me Briones has always been charming, but I remember one day in particular when the land seemed to reach out to me and become almost excruciatingly alive. I was hiking along, rucksack on my back, thoughtless and casual, when I heard a very distant, mournful, whistling sound. It was an eerie, monotonous song, and every so often the pitch would change. It seemed to be coming from everywhere at once.

For a long time this hollow, haunting song followed me along the trail. Were there Sirens here such as sang to Ulysses and his men? Was it the keening of the widow Briones for her dead husband? Was it the singing of a Costanoan Indian for his lost land, his lost language, his utter extinguishment? Was it the song of the land itself?

I found this distant whistling to be infinitely sad and infinitely beautiful. It was the song of the trees, the grasses, the soil, and all the strange, beautiful, and tragic people who once lived here. It was a simple song that flowed through the branches of the oaks, around the high peaks, between the blades of grass, back through the past and out into the future, through my mind and beyond —— a lonesome, lovely song that was wrapping everything together in a thin strong blanket of sound.

I feel almost foolish telling you how the song ended. I reached into my rucksack for my canteen. When I turned the cap of the canteen the song popped and abruptly ceased. It had been air seeping in through a narrow opening of the canteen cap. I felt slightly chagrined, but still elated. The singer may have been a faulty canteen cap. But what remains with me is the feeling of enchantment that the song had drawn out of the land and laid before me like a precious gift —— an enchantment that is a real and rightful part of Briones Park.

Anthony Chabot

Anthony Chabot Regional Park is a huge, 4,000 acre park in the hills above East Oakland and San Leandro. It has vast acres of grassland, brush, oak-bay forests, eucalyptus forests, and even some redwood forests —— all spread out in a leisurely, generous fashion and crisscrossed by a few wide horse trails. A very few horse trails, in fact. Most of Anthony Chabot has no trails at all. The grasslands and the more open forests are yours to wander over, but the dense brushland is almost totally inaccessible to any one larger than a fox or a brush rabbit. This impenetrable brush is the last true wilderness remaining in the city of Oakland.

Throughout this sprawling, wild land the Park District has placed several "attractions:" picnic areas, group camping areas, a family campground (see page 99). a rifle range, an archery range, the 315-acre Lake Chabot (see page 76), an area of motorcycle trails, and an equestrian center that rents horses.

But despite the hodge-podge of attractions, Anthony Chabot has a peculiar quietness of its own. It has many exquisite nooks and canyons where you can hide from the 20th century. My favorite is Bird Watchers' Trail, a mile long, very narrow intimate loop trail that runs off MacDonald Trail near MacDonald Gate. The trail follows a bouncing creek, and it is a botanical circus of rare and beautiful plants.

Another private nook is Buckeye Canyon, a small box canyon whose entrance is behind the row of eucalyptus trees at the north end of Big Trees. Buckeye Canyon is Irish-green and magical in the early spring with its growth of glistening mosses and ferns. If you poke around here you may find the remains of an old cistern that supplied water to a ranch that was at Big Trees during the last century.

There are other hidden corners in Anthony Chabot, and if you spend a few days wandering around you'll surely discover more of your own. And like the rest of California Anthony Chabot is unbelievably beautiful in the green-grass, flower-speckled spring. But I cannot pretend that Anthony Chabot as a whole is a truly spectacular park. It doesn't reach out and grab you with its prettiness the way some of the lakes do, nor does it overwhelm you with its grandeur the way Redwood, Briones, Las Trampas, or Sunol sometimes do. The scenery here is understated. I know it's iconoclastic for me to admit this —— we nature freaks are supposed to be in a constant state of ecstacy, alive at every pore, vibrating like bees —— but one day I even found myself *bored*. I had been to Anthony Chabot dozens of times, and the park had become for me as stale as old beer, when I turned a corner and noticed a fox sitting in the trail. The fox got up and walked ahead of me, imitating my dispirited shuffle, throwing occasional glances back at me to make sure I was watching. I stopped in amazement. The fox lay down in the middle of the trail, curled up its body, nestled its nose into its tail, and looked at me with pitying eyes. When I moved closer the fox reluctantly arose, moved on a few more yards, and curled up again to look at me some more. Then suddenly it disappeared into the brush. The trail was empty again, but a feeling of cleanness and newness swept over me that I cannot explain. I had seen many foxes before, but this was the first fox I had ever really *seen*.

In some ways Anthony Chabot has become for me like a modest theater I once went to. The staging, the acoustics, and the seating were all sort of ordinary. But it was here that I saw some of the most exciting plays I've ever seen. That's how it's been with Anthony Chabot. Here more than anywhere else I have had the experience of cracking through what I've been programmed to see and catching a glimpse of the world beyond. It happened at the unexpected sight of a flower that seemed to cut into me so deeply I got scared; in a vulture's mid-flight wobble that seemed to last forever; in the plunge of a hawk so precipitous that the bottom seemed to have fallen out of the earth; and in the curious wrap-around and swish of the fox's tail as he stared at me with pitying eyes. There were times at Anthony Chabot when the murkiness of ordinary perception lifted and I felt that I could see things directly, immediately —— as they really are.

But whatever I might think of Anthony Chabot at present, I know that if I return in another twenty or thirty years I'll have to revise my opinion. Anthony Chabot is undergoing a profound ecological change. It had always been predominantly grassland. Aerial photos from before 1942 (when the Park District acquired the land) show vast areas of grass and only about 275 acres of brush in the whole park. Twenty years later, in 1963, another survey found the grassland disappearing and there were then 750 acres of brush. Brush has been creeping over "Grass

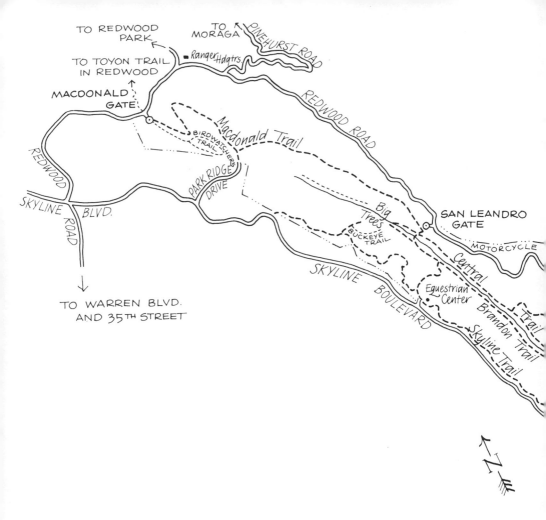

TO REDWOOD
PARK

TO
MORAGA

PINEHURST ROAD

TO TOYON TRAIL
IN REDWOOD

Ranger Hdqtrs.

MACDONALD
GATE

REDWOOD ROAD

BIRDWATCHERS TRAIL

Macdonald Trail

REDWOOD ROAD

SKYLINE
ROAD

PARK RIDGE DRIVE

SKYLINE BLVD.

Big Trees

San Leandro Gate → SAN LEANDRO GATE

BUCKEYE TRAIL

MOTORCYCLE

TO WARREN BLVD.
AND 35TH STREET

SKYLINE BOULEVARD

Equestrian Center

Central

Brandon Trail

Skyline Trail

Trail

N

Legend

PAVED ROAD	═══
HIKING & RIDING	- - - -
FOOTPATH	– – – –
STREAM	～～
PARK BOUNDARY	–·–·–
PARKING LOT	⊙
STONE SHELTER	🏠
PICNIC AREA	⛺

scale of miles

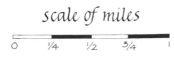

0   ¼   ½   ¾   1

ANTHONY CHABOT
LAKE CHABOT

4,750 acres

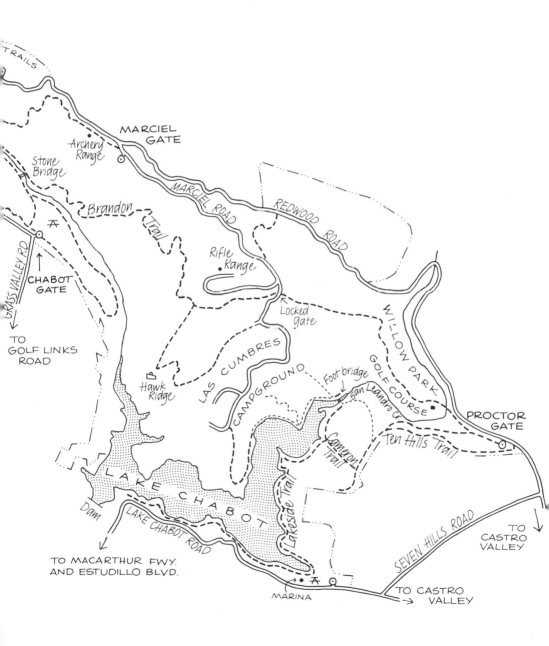

TRAILS

MARCIEL GATE

Archery Range

Stone Bridge

MARCIEL ROAD

REDWOOD ROAD

Brandon *Trail*

GRASS VALLEY RD.

CHABOT GATE

Rifle Range

TO GOLF LINKS ROAD

Locked gate

WILLOW PARK

Hawk Ridge

LAS CUMBRES

CAMPGROUND

Footbridge

San Leandro Cr.

GOLF COURSE

PROCTOR GATE

Cameron Trail

Ten Hills Trail

LAKE CHABOT

Dam

LAKESIDE ROAD

Lakeside Trail

SEVEN HILLS ROAD

TO CASTRO VALLEY

TO MACARTHUR FWY. AND ESTUDILLO BLVD.

MARINA

TO CASTRO VALLEY

Valley" (as this area was once called) at the rate of nearly twenty-five acres a year. (Similar invasions are taking place at Redwood Park and Tilden.)

Many theories exist to explain why the brush is taking over. Some say it's because fire has been over-controlled, and the grasslands need periodic fires to keep them grassy. Others feel that the exclusion of grazing is the major factor since cattle tend to trample and browse young brush. Still others insist that the basic cause is the change of grasses in this area: European annual grasses have replaced the deep-rooted native perennials which might have held the land better. Most likely all of these factors play some part.

Also, the species of brush leading the invasion, coyote brush, is admirably equipped to take over the meadows. A relative of the aster, coyote brush has composite flowers —— the latest, most improved invention of the plant kingdom. Its seeds are numerous and float great distances on little parachutes. If you dig up a coyote brush you'll see that its roots are extensive and greedy, often three times as deep as the plant is tall. Rub your fingers over the leaf, and you'll feel a waxy covering, cutin, that protects the leaf by preventing the hot sun from burning the tender cells deeper within.

Some ecologists and recreation administrators bemoan the loss of meadowland. And with good reason. Meadows are a lot more fun to look at and play on than brush. They also support more wildflowers. Nevertheless, the brush environment is not without its virtues. It provides food and shelter for innumerable small animals and birds; and the current mixture of grass, brush, and forest at Anthony Chabot is probably the best possible environment for wildlife.

But even the victory of the brush is only a temporary victory. Built into the marvellous mechanisms of the coyote brush is a tragic flaw: as the patches of brush get thicker and thicker, denser and denser, they shade the ground below them more and more. Within this shade no other coyote brush can grow: the filtered sunlight is not strong enough to penetrate the thick cutinous layer of wax on the leaves. But the seedlings of other plants are better adapted to the shade. Within the older stands of coyote brush you can often see elderberry, oak, bay, madrone, and the other trees and bushes that will make up the hardwood forests of the future. In another 100 years people will wonder why in the world this forested area was once called "Grass Valley."

What does it all mean? I used to walk through Chabot Park with a group of friends studying the changes that were taking place and noticing how the wildlife was adapting. One of my friends, Charlie, used to look at everything and ask precisely that question: "What does it all mean?" At first we thought the question was amusing, but after a while he was asking it several times a day.

He asked it of the coyote brush, the monkey flowers, the oak trees, and the blades of grass.

"What does it all mean?" he demanded to know, as if a great cosmic secret were hiding behind every leaf.

Soon we got very tired of hearing the same question. One day we pulled Charlie aside and gently explained the facts of life: "Look, Charlie, friend, it really doesn't mean a whole lot. You know: a grass is a grass, a flower is a flower, a bee is a bee (which is really part of a flower), a tree is a tree. Things are what they are."

Charlie thought about it for a few days. The next time we went hiking he no longer asked, "What does it all mean?" He merely looked wide-eyed at all the marvellous goings on around him and said, "Hello."

We all thought it was quite an improvement.

Garin Ranch

Garin Regional Park in the Hayward Hills was formerly a ranch that belonged to the Garin Family. It is still grazed by cattle, and it feels so authentically like a private ranch that hiking here is almost as good as trespassing. In fact I've heard of one veteran hiker who refuses to enter through the park gate, but instead wiggles underneath the barbed wire fence —— just for old times' sake.

On the whole Garin Ranch is nothing more than an ordinary, honest piece of ranchland that has somehow managed to stay out of the way of the 20th century. It is 473 acres of mostly meadowland with a few deeply wooded canyons. In the spring, wildflowers throw themselves madly over the hilltops. Flocks of warblers arrive, twinkling among the bushes like Christmas lights. In the shady canyons the buds of the big-leaf maples burst open with a noiseless fireworks shower of leaves and blossoms. At night the ground squirrels and rabbits cower in their holes, while foxes prowl through the starry grass and coyotes howl at the moon.

To get a clear idea of how Garin Ranch relates to the rest of the East Bay, climb to the top of one of its peaks. To the west you'll see the flatlands of Hayward, Newark, and Fremont covered with factories, houses, shopping centers, and freeways. To the east you'll notice recent housing developments that are creeping over the hills. Garin Ranch is gradually being surrounded by development. At Garin you're not getting away from it all as much as you're getting on top of it all. Garin Ranch is the penthouse garden of Hayward —— a penthouse garden with a thriving wildlife population.

Much of the wildlife here begins with a tiny plant called filaree. Filaree has a five-petalled, violet flower with a red stem. You may not notice it unless you stick your nose cow-like in between the cold, green blades of grass. After a while you'll discover that the grasslands around Garin are dotted with these little flowers.

Although the flowers are inconspicuous, filaree seeds have a way of making themselves very well known. At first they look like spears, with pointed heads and more or less straight shafts. But as the humidity changes, different parts of the "shaft" expand and contract at differing rates. The shaft now curls up into a spiral or cork-screw, providing a motion whereby the seed twists itself into the ground —— or in-to one's socks, as every hiker soon discovers.

Not only does filaree turn itself into an amazing seed, but even more incredible it can turn itself into a ground squirrel. Filaree is the staff of life for thousands of these little animals who live on Garin Ranch.

Ground squirrels love ranch life. In fact they have even prospered with the com-ing of Europeans. The newcomers plowed up the hard clayey soil and planted wheat and other delicious grains. They also introduced exotic plants, like filaree and like the heavy seeding annual grasses. Ground squirrels, like many other epicures, came to prefer these delectable imported foods over the domestic varieties. At the same time the Europeans short-sightedly reduced the populations of coyotes, eagles, and other natural predators that had kept the squirrel population within reasonable bounds.

From a fairly insignificant animal among California's fauna, the ground squirrel population burgeoned. They became a major agricultural pest until the 1920's, when

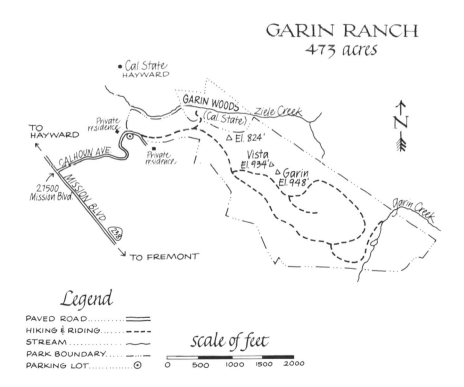

GARIN RANCH
473 acres

Legend

PAVED ROAD
HIKING & RIDING
STREAM
PARK BOUNDARY
PARKING LOT

scale of feet

0   500   1000   1500   2000

the inflated population was hit by a plague. Authorities declared them a health hazard. Schools in California were recessed for the day to allow children to get out and kill ground squirrels. Games, competitions, and trophies were organized around the slaughter. Posters were hung in public places, showing President Hoover urging American youth: "Do your patriotic duty. Kill a ground squirrel."

The extermination campaign was disastrous, at least for the people who partook in it. A whole generation was convinced that ground squirrels are dirty, harmful animals. In fact there are still many thousands of people who cannot bring themselves to enjoy these lively, clownish, inquisitive little creatures.

As to whether the campaign had much effect on the ground squirrels, any one who has ever tried to get rid of mice, rats, or any other rodent knows the answer. Some marginal colonies were destroyed. But by and large the ground squirrels showed such enthusiasm for reproduction that whatever vacancies were created in their ranks were filled quite effortlessly in a few years.

Today the squirrel population at Garin Ranch is large and prosperous. They run along their paths, dive into their holes, and return to chirp at an intruder with great gusto. I personally feel that they have a superb sense of humor, but I won't push that point. In any case, they lead public lives and are great fun to watch.

Many predators have been attracted to Garin by the ground squirrels, and paradoxically they benefit the squirrel population by keeping them alert and plague-free. At odd hours you might see a badger here, savagely and single-mindedly excavating a squirrel hole. At dawn or dusk you might happen upon a coyote looking sharply and intelligently over a field before racing off to follow whatever ground squirrel smell is pulling so insistently at its nose. During the day the air is full of hawks swooping low to caress the contours of the hills. Once after a fire left a ground squirrel colony unusually exposed, as many as eight golden eagles were counted at one time, assembling at Garin to share the easy hunting.

The chain that begins with filaree and ends with coyotes and eagles is only one of the many wildlife chains that run through Garin Ranch. Other chains are formed by mice, rabbits, quail, skunks, snakes, raccoons, foxes, and ultimately vultures. Together they make up the thriving wildlife of Garin Ranch.

A very good piece of news is that the East Bay Regional Park District is going to acquire the Meyers Ranch immediately to the south of Garin. This, along with

Garin Woods, a natural area owned by Cal State, will make up a large, exciting park in the Hayward Hills.

Yet at the current rate of development, it is likely that within a decade or two even this enlarged park will be ringed by houses, and cut off from the wild lands that stretch to the east. If this park does indeed become cut off like an island, what will happen to the wildlife here? I'm not sure. But I hope that wide corridors can be maintained to connect Garin with the rest of the natural world so that we'll be spared the pain of having to find out.

Huckleberry Preserve

 Huckleberry Botanic Preserve is a unique and distinguished community of plants in the Oakland Hills. Here you will find a dwarf forest of rare shrubs and bushes, and a narrow footpath that threads almost apologetically for one mile through the Preserve.

The land all around Huckleberry Preserve has been altered. It has been planted to Australian blue gum eucalyptus trees, terraced by sheep trails, taken over by European grasses, sectioned off by paved roadways, and dotted by houses. Even the redwoods to the south and west have been logged once, twice, or even three times, and are only now beginning to show off with a hint of their former majesty. But Huckleberry Preserve is a brave little piece of land that has never been conquered. Those hardy, scrubby, untamed bushes, as rigid as bone and as alive as fire, are a completely authentic remnant of native California.

Whenever I think of Huckleberry Preserve a very specific scene comes to mind. It is a crisp, clear winter's day, and I am sitting just above the trail. My breath condenses into puffs of smoke. My hands are pushed into my pockets. I am looking at the blue sky through a gnarled, twisted manzanita bush. Its leaves are stiff and waxy, its pink-white flowers dangle like miniature Grecian vases, and its polished red stem is writhing against the sky like a lick of flame. Just then two courting hummingbirds whizz by, and I know that they are sparks in the cold winter sky.

But flowers and hummingbirds in the middle of winter? Certainly, for Huckleberry Preserve has a climate of its own. It has something to do with the eastern exposure, the edge of the fog belt, and the mechanics of inversion layering. Here, spring does not wait stubbornly until March or April. It sometimes comes as early as Christmas, and it's always in full swing by February. On many a gloomy winter's day I've found spring hiding out shyly at the Preserve, and I've raced back to town with the message to all my house-bound friends: "Spring is alive and well at Huckleberry Preserve." The bell-like manzanita flowers are blooming. On the leatherwood the buds have burst and the lemon-yellow flowers are spilling out. Currants, roses, thimbleberries, and other plants are flowering, and knowledgeable Bay Area hummingbirds have gathered for the magnificent mid-winter feast.

Huckleberry Preserve is also out of step with the rest of the Bay Area in late summer and early fall. Elsewhere it's hot and dry, and even the most ardent nature lover usually limits his explorations to the latest issue of Audubon Magazine. But August through October is nut and berry season at the Preserve: huckleberries by the ton, manzanita berries, hazelnuts, chinquapin nuts, silktassel berries, currants, snowberries, nightshade berries —— millions of fat berries and nuts that create a sort of Grossinger's for the local birds.

Huckleberry Preserve has also been a sort of Grossinger's for local naturalists. In 1915 W. L. Jepson, a famous biologist, noted: "This is always an inspiring botanizing ground." And Huckleberry Preserve has been turning on botanists ever since. If you want to find out what excites them so much, here is a sampling:

....Western leatherwood (*Dirca occidentalis),* a plant with pliant, leathery branches that is found only here, a few other places in the East Bay, and nowhere else in the world.

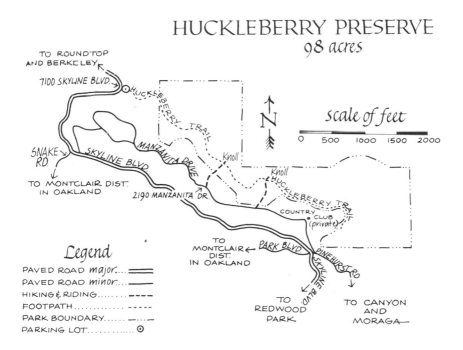

HUCKLEBERRY PRESERVE
98 acres

....Huckleberries, so common on the Preserve, but not found anywhere else in the East Bay except in scattered patches near Redwood Peak.

....A manzanita called *Arctostaphylos Andersoni* var. *pallida* which is said to be unique to this one area.

....Another rare manzanita, *Arctostaphylos crustacea.*

....Silktassel *(Garrya elliptica),* chinquapin, and wild iris, all common on the Preserve, yet fairly rare elsewhere in the Bay Area.

....Plus many more bushes, trees, ferns, and flowers. (Many of these plants are described in Roxana Ferris's book, *Native Shrubs of the San Francisco Bay Area,* put out by the University of California Press and on sale almost everywhere for $2.65.)

This natural community of rare plants makes Huckleberry Preserve one of the most significant botanical areas in California. But don't let that scare you away. Despite the importance of the place, I must confess that many a plump huckleberry has disappeared down my throat —— and (if the truth be known) down the throats of some of California's most illustrious preservationists. Huckleberry Preserve does not have a hushed, don't-touch, museum air about it. The intimate mile-long footpath that passes through the Preserve's cool bay forests and through its electrical brushland provides you with a joyous hiking experience. There are views of Flicker Ridge nearby and Las Trampas Ridge to the southeast, while Mount Diablo staggers and swells in the distance. And because the trail is small, level, and lined with luscious huckleberries it is a very fine trail indeed for little kids.

The East Bay Regional Park District is now in the process of purchasing the Preserve from private owners —— a process that was vastly accelerated when one of the owners began bulldozing some of the area for homesites. Since the purchasing is not yet completed no one is sure how many acres will be included in the Preserve, or what regulations will be enforced. The map on the preceding page shows what are presently the two major access routes.

According to the long term plans of the Park District, Huckleberry Trail is to be part of a thirty mile trail that will take ambitious hikers from Richmond to Castro Valley. This is far in the future, though.

I've visited Huckleberry Preserve perhaps twenty times, and I've developed an extraordinary affection for it. In other East Bay Parks I feel dwarfed by the landscape around me. But at Huckleberry Preserve I often feel like a giant striding through a diminutive forest. Other parks usually leave me feeling softer, gentler, mellower. It's the effect of the gentle, rolling hills, the submissive meadows, the noble forests. But at Huckleberry Preserve there is something bracing and energizing about these gnarled, strong bushes, the hardness of their branches, the distinctness and crispness of everything, the unconquered history of the area.

To the Indians the land was full of gods and spirits, and they would go to special mountains, springs, hills, or rivers to court specific types of experiences and powers. Similarly, I visit Huckleberry Preserve for something rarer than a rare shrub —— for the feeling of clarity, sharpness, and strength this land bestows on those who become intimate with it.

Kennedy Grove

 Kennedy Grove (named in memory of John F. Kennedy) is a small, 100-acre park near the base of the San Pablo Reservoir Dam. With its picnic areas and trimmed lawns it is very much like a city park.

What makes Kennedy Grove remarkable are the handsome, young, blue-gum eucalyptus trees that shade the picnic areas. These trees were planted by the Water Company in 1910. They are originally from Australia, and like other Australian natives (kangaroos, koala bears, and platypuses) eucalyptus trees are rather strange. They have straight hard trunks, shredding bark, and long curved leaves that smell like Vick's Cough Drops. Branches come crashing to the ground without warning —— often on warm, windless summer days.

At the turn of the century eucalyptus was the get-rich-quick tree of California. Millions were planted until the eucalyptus bubble burst in 1911, leaving 50,000 acres of weird Australian trees to fend for themselves in the California environment. (For more on the history of the East Bay eucalyptus boom, see page 36.)

How has California wildlife adapted to this strange, new environment? "Badly," claim many experts. Early in my California education they explained to me that eucalyptus forests are "wildlife deserts." So for many years I hiked through these forests quickly, because obviously there was nothing to see. And sure enough, I saw nothing. The less I saw the more I hurried, the more I hurried the less I saw, until after a while I found that I too could verify the "wildlife desert" theory from my own experience.

One day I was expounding the fine points of this theory to a naturalist friend of mine. And to my utter amazement my friend began to speak heresies. He talked about the insects, spiders, rodents, and snakes that he regularly finds hiding beneath the litterfall. He talked about the hawks and owls that use the trees for roosts and for nests. He told me that certain squirrels had even developed a taste for the pungent eucalyptus berries. The more he talked, the more intrigued I got.

The next time I walked in a eucalyptus forest, instead of speeding through it I slowed down. I looked around, turned over logs, listened keenly, and sat down in inconspicuous places to watch the goings on. I noticed how little birds were building nests under the furls of bark on the trees, and under one furl I once discovered a sleepy, confused bat. Among the tree tops I noticed the blue jays who were forever carrying on their family squabbles. I saw juncos and towhees picking over the ground, and in the spring I saw how the swarms of bees attracted to the eucalyptus flowers were themselves attracting the attention of shrikes and other insect-eating birds. I also noticed a squirrel tasting a eucalyptus berry, and I saw where mice had girdled a young eucalyptus sapling by eating off the bark. At night I heard the cracklings and stirrings of hundreds of unseen animals. In truth I have found the eucalyptus forest to be a fairly rich and exciting place, as these strange Australian trees and the familiar California wildlife work out a relationship that is brand new in the history of the world.

Besides the eucalyptus forest, Kennedy Grove bears the signs of still another grand scale commercial venture that didn't pan out. The California and Nevada Railroad, chartered in the 1880's, ran through the middle of the park. Its ambitious owners intended it to run from Emeryville to the mines of Utah and Nevada, but, alas, it never got past Orinda. The trip from Emeryville was apparently very pleasant, as the narrow-gauge train carried its load of farmers and sightseers through the San Pablo Creek Valley. But the return trip was somewhat embarrassing. Because there was no turntable at the end of the line, the train had to run backwards all the way from Orinda to the Bay.

Two picnic areas in Kennedy Grove are named after nearby stops on the railroad: Frenchman's Curve and Clancy's Place.

What does the future hold for Kennedy Grove? Many of the crowded eucalyptus trees have been thinned out as part of the design of the picnic area, and the ground is irrigated to keep the lawns green. I imagine that in another fifty or sixty years the thinning and the steady watering will result in some of the most magnificent and massive eucalyptus in the state.

In the age of the iron horse, picnickers reached this area by train. Now they arrive by car. But if the signs are right, and we are at last reaching the end of the automobile age, I imagine that a new fate awaits Kennedy Grove. Once automobile traffic thins out (or bicycle trails are built) San Pablo Dam Road will certainly become one of the most popular biking routes in the Bay Area. It stretches from Richmond to Orinda, and is nearly level and mostly undeveloped all the way. By the time the eucalyptus here reach heroic proportions, I expect that Kennedy Grove will be a favorite stopping place for thousands of cyclists.*

*Not quite! Since mid-1974 the park has been open only to groups with reservations. Call 531-9043 for more information.

Redwood

Look at the map on page 34, and you'll see that Redwood Park is shaped a lot like a mushroom —— a 2,000 acre magical mushroom of grassland, brush, and peaceful redwood forests.

I worked at this magical mushroom of a park for nearly three years, and I only dimly remember the initial impact the quiet, somber redwood forest made on me. "Are you *sure* this is Oakland?" I kept asking the fellow I was working with. But after several hundred (perhaps thousand) miles of hiking through Redwood Park I learned that Oakland is not just East 14th Street or the gigantic pinball machine that the downtown area has become. It's also a place where you can find clumps of mushrooms, marmalade orange and sulphur yellow, glowing softly in the leaf litter of a dark forest. Where one night I counted twenty-three deer browsing on a single meadow, and where there are innumerable foxes, racoons, skunks, possums, owls, and hawks. Where Douglas irises get dressed up like cocky young noblemen in cloaks and plumes for their annual spring ball. Where on hot summer days vultures circle high above the forests and meadows, describing lazy helixes toward the sun. But most of all it is where there stands a vast forest of redwoods, lofty trees five to six feet in diameter and over 100 feet tall. Very few hikers seem to know about this forest, and those who do are small insignificant figures as they walk under the towering canopy, among the straight columns of the trunks, and through the gentle, nourishing gloom of the redwood forest.

The forest looks ancient and permanent. Yet in fact the redwoods at Redwood Park are all youngsters, less than a century old. They are a race of adolescent giants rising out of the logged-off remains of what was perhaps the most magnificent grove of redwoods the world has ever seen.

As far as I know there are no records of what the original forest was like. Apparently grizzly bears and condors were fairly common. The trees were so immense

30

that some of them were clearly visible from the Golden Gate sixteen miles away. In the days before lighthouses and buoys, ships entering the Bay used to line up with these landmark trees to avoid certain shoals.

But by the early 1850's the redwood forest was logged clean. The wood went into building Benicia, Martinez, Oakland, and San Francisco. The redwood forest became "a sea of stumps." But even the stumps were extraordinary. John Muir, Asa Gray, and Joshua Whitney (after whom Mount Whitney was named) were among the notables of that time who visited these "melancholy ruins" to marvel at the remains. Many of the stumps measured more than twenty feet across. One stump near the summit of Redwood Peak measured thirty-three and a half feet in diameter, and may have been the largest redwood ever known. By comparison the largest (in diameter) redwood alive today is the Stout Tree in Jedediah Smith State Park, a mere twenty feet.

In the following decades, however, even the stumps were not to be spared. Woodchoppers swarmed over the hills, hacking down the stumps and grubbing out the roots for firewood. During the 1870's and 1880's the stumps supplied over half the firewood in the East Bay. And the trees which did resprout were cut down once more after 1906 to help rebuild San Francisco after the earthquake.

After the logging came a pastoral interlude in the history of Redwood Park, as settlers arrived with their cattle and their small farms. What is now the ranger headquarters on Redwood Road was once the schoolhouse of these early settlers. Old Church Picnic Area was the site of their church. And even today you can find throughout the park the remains of their orchards —— pear trees, apple trees, and plum trees that flower brilliantly each spring and still bear delicious fruit. The settlers were gradually moved out in the 1920's when the Water Company took over the land as watershed. In the mid 1930's the Water Company passed the land on to the newly formed East Bay Regional Park District.

In the late 1930's W. P. A. crews arrived on the scene and built many of the roads and trails and erected the four stone huts that are scattered along Stream Trail. During the Second World War the Park was used freely by various military units. Naval Air Cadets "lived off the land" —— eating berries and trapping small game as part of their survival training. A camouflage unit complete with cannons, tanks, bazookas, and half-tracks played eerie games of hide-and-seek in the redwood forests. Strangest of all were the burial crews of 1,500 men who would set up a two-acre simulated cemetery complete with fencing, a signed entrance, and 500 white crosses. Every two weeks a bulldozer would blade the area clean, and a new crew would arrive to repeat the macabre process.

Finally, the Park District itself has made minor efforts to "develop" parts of Red-

31

wood Park. Redwood Canyon is now a popular picnic area. Barricades, jumps, and an exhibition ring have been erected on Hunt Field for the equestrian set. And Roberts Recreation Area maintains a noisy, happy, high-energy mood throughout the summer with its heated outdoor swimming pool, children's playground and wading pool, and its redwood-shaded picnic tables.

This, then, has been the strange history of Redwood Park. But fortunately the latest chapter is being written once more by the trees. Despite the logging, the stump cutting, the root grubbing, the re-logging, the settling, the grazing, and the exploits of the military, despite all that has happened to the land, the redwood trees have grown back once more. No wonder they are called *sempervirens* ——— always living.

Today the trees are less than 100 years old, but they have already regained their air of dignity and permanence. With their great size and their racial memories that stretch back 100 million years to the Age of Reptiles, the redwoods at Redwood Park seem once again aloof from the modern world. The leaf litter and thick duff have carpeted the forest floor, and it takes a practiced eye to find signs of the previous logging. Now and then hikers find old ox-shoes or bits of metal from axes and saws. Flat areas (such as Millsite) mark the location of old sawmills. And hikers through the park, especially along Stream Trail, may spot old "skid roads," grooves gouged into the hillside that were originally greased with animal fat and along which the enormous logs were dragged.

Another sign of the logging is the way the trees grow. Throughout the forest most of the trees are arranged in small circles ——— like groups of oversized kids playing ring-around-a-rosey. In the center of each circle is the ghost of a tree that grew over 100 years ago. Once the tree was felled, sprouting took place around the edges of the stump. The great size of some of these "family circles," as they are called, hints at how enormous the original trees once were ——— and suggests the great future in store for this land if we leave things alone for the next few thousand years.

In addition to its massive redwood forest Redwood Park also has many hundreds of acres of grassland, brush, and (besides the redwoods) no fewer than three distinct forest environments. These other areas are so vast that I have known people who have hiked all day at Redwood Park without ever having set foot in a redwood grove. Near the northern corner of the park, above Girl's Camp, is an extensive eucalyptus forest. Around Orchard Trail is a huge oak-bay-madrone forest ——— dense, even impenetrable, and especially rich in wildlife. And a forest of Monterey pines can be found near the junction of West Ridge and French Trails. These pines were planted decades ago, perhaps to replace the logged-off redwoods. Misplaced natives of the Monterey Peninsula, they are now old and decayed, leaning precariously, their tops broken off by the winds. There is a gothic air about them, an air of defeated nobility, that makes this one of the most haunting areas of Redwood Park.

And finally there are the creeks that bounce and bubble in the spring, the grassland that forms intimate sunlit clearings in the forests and in the brush, and the remains of old orchards that reward the diligent hiker with an occasional handful of plums.

There's grandeur and variety in these hills, only a busride away from downtown Oakland, making Redwood Park one of the best hiking parks in the East Bay. Judging from the moss-covered initials and dates carved into the rocks of Redwood Peak, hiking has been popular since the turn of the century. And considering the way the redwoods have been growing, it will undoubtedly be even more popular in the centuries to come.

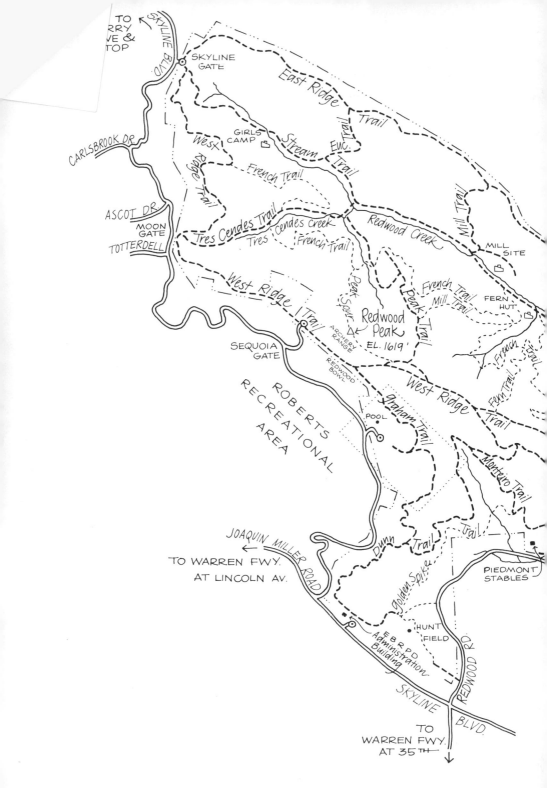

TO
RRY
VE &
TOP

SKYLINE BLVD

SKYLINE GATE

East Ridge Trail

CARLSBROOK DR.

West Ridge Trail

GIRLS CAMP

Stream Trail

Euc. Trail

Mill Trail

French Trail

ASCOT DR.

MOON GATE

TOTTERDELL

Tres Cendes Trail

Tres Cendes Creek

Redwood Creek

MILL SITE

French Trail

Peak Spur

Peak Trail

French Trail

Mill Trail

FERN HUT

West Ridge Trail

SEQUOIA GATE

Redwood Peak

EL. 1619'

ARCHERY RANGE

Fern Trail

French Trail

ROBERTS

RECREATIONAL

AREA

REDWOOD BOWL

West Ridge

POOL

Graham Trail

Monteiro Trail

JOAQUIN MILLER ROAD

TO WARREN FWY.
AT LINCOLN AV.

Dunn Trail

Trail

Golden Spike

PIEDMONT STABLES

HUNT FIELD

E B R P D
Administration
Building

SKYLINE BLVD.

REDWOOD RD.

TO
WARREN FWY.
AT 35TH

34

REDWOOD
2,162 acres

Legend

PAVED ROAD.......... ═══
HIKING & RIDING........ ▬ ▬ ▬
FOOTPATH............... - - - - -
STREAM................. ⌁
PARK BOUNDARY...... ▬ ᴗ ▬
PARKING LOT........... ⊙
STONE SHELTER....... 🏠
PICNIC AREA........... ⩜

N ↑

scale of miles

0   ¼   ½   ¾   1

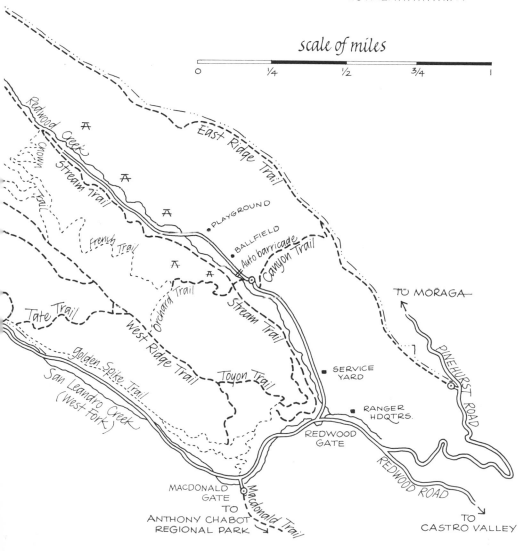

Redwood Creek
Crown Trail
Stream Trail
East Ridge Trail
French Trail
PLAYGROUND
BALLFIELD
Auto barricade
Canyon Trail
TO MORAGA
Orchard Trail
Stream Trail
Tate Trail
West Ridge Trail
Golden Spike Trail
Toyon Trail
SERVICE YARD
PINEHURST ROAD
San Leandro Creek (West Fork)
RANGER HDQTRS.
REDWOOD GATE
MACDONALD GATE
TO ANTHONY CHABOT REGIONAL PARK
Macdonald Trail
REDWOOD ROAD
TO CASTRO VALLEY

Roundtop

Roundtop is a small, stoop-shouldered peak in the Oakland Hills. It is only 1,761 feet high, and you would hardly guess that it was once the most prominent volcano in the East Bay.

About ten million years ago a freshwater lake extended from what is now Tilden Park to the site of the San Leandro Reservoir. The volcano was born under the waters of this lake. When the lava stopped flowing, sediments from the lake settled over the lava deposits. Then volcanic activity began again. Geologists have counted eleven separate lava flows and at least two violent explosions in the birth of Roundtop. In the millions of years that followed, the alternating volcanic and sedimentary layers were folded, tilted, crumpled, and tossed about so that today Roundtop is one of the favorite stomping grounds for local geologists in search of complexity.

After its traumatic birth you might imagine that Roundtop has settled down into the shabby retirement you'd expect from a worn-out volcano. Far from it. In this century alone Roundtop has been changing identities with the startling rapidity of a model at a fashion show.

Early in the century Roundtop was a round, grassy, treeless hill. From 1910 until 1973 it was covered by a dense, thriving eucalyptus forest. Now, however, the eucalytus are mostly gone, and today the peak is carpeted with thick green grasses, poppies, lupines, and sage brush. A few Monterey pines are scattered over the broad slopes, and thousands of meadow wildflowers celebrate the death of the eucalyptus with unconcealed merriment. I wish the wildflowers well, but I wonder how much longer they can celebrate. For there are already signs that Roundtop is about to undergo still more dramatic changes in the near future.

Roundtop has been officially named Sibley Regional Park after Robert Sibley, one of the founders of the East Bay Regional Park District. But the man who set in motion the sweeping changes here was Frank Havens, a turn-of-the-century millionaire and founder of the Mahogany Eucalyptus and Land Company. The purpose of this grandiose, ill-conceived company was to cover the crests of the Oakland-Berkeley Hills with great forests of eucalyptus trees. As Havens put it, eucalyptus was "the most valuable tree on the face of the globe. No teak, mahogany, ebony, hickory, or oak was ever tougher, denser, stronger or of more glorious hardness," he declared in a prospectus to potential stockholders. Not only did he promise riches, but he promised them fast, claiming that a eucalyptus sapling might grow five or six inches in a single day!

Between 1910 and 1913 Havens lured thousands of investors. He set up nine nurseries and an arboretum, and he employed as many as 200 men at one time. Eucalyptus by the million were were planted along the fourteen-mile stretch from North Berkeley to what is now Redwood Park. Roundtop was at the center of Haven's empire, and it was Havens who had Skyline Boulevard built as a scenic drive to connect his various real estate and lumber holdings in the Oakland Hills. These were big ventures, and to give Havens credit he undoubtedly believed in the infallibility of his eucalyptus empire. In 1913 he invited a forester to test-mill a few eucalyptus. And then he learned the terrible truth: the blue gum eucalyptus he had planted were worthless. It turned out that blue gum was never used for lumber in Australia, and the species of eucalyptus that the Australians did use were so slow growing that the trees could not be harvested until they were several hundred years old.

I don't know the name of the forester Havens invited to test the eucalyptus, but some one ought to erect a monument in his honor. If he had found that eucalyptus was even half as valuable as Havens claimed, today the East Bay Hills would be the scene of one of the most massive logging operations in the world. The failure of blue gum eucalyptus to produce good lumber is one of the luckiest things that has happened to the environment of the East Bay.

After the bubble burst, the eucalyptus forests were left alone. They were never thinned or in any way tended. They grew weedy and thick, creating one of the eeriest environments in the world. California wildlife began to mix with these exotic trees, and a brand new community developed (see page 28).

Throughout most of this century Roundtop has been one of the most impenetrable and least explored of the eucalyptus forests in the East Bay Hills. In the long, slow summer of 1973 you would hardly have expected Roundtop to make headline news. The trees stood tall and stringy. The undergrowth was a jungle of brush and litterfall. Leaves shimmered idly in the sun. On hot summer days you could sometimes feel the troubled wind searching out the eucalyptus grove as a place to rest and sleep. At dusk a sudden stirring of the leaves and a creaking of the trunks announced that the winds were arousing themselves again, gathering themselves together like a caravan that would soon depart and leave the night-time forest strangely silent. These eucalyptus forests seemed as unchangeable as the hills themselves.

But in the winter of 1972-73 subfreezing weather struck the Bay Area and injured the eucalyptus trees. Roundtop with its high, exposed location was among the most severely damaged. The leaves died back and most of the trees seemed dead. Experts warned that these vast forests of dead and injured trees presented an extraordinary fire hazard, and newspapers spread images of fires roaring down the hills to consume the cities and towns along the Bay.

In the spring of 1973 it was decided that the eucalyptus forests would have to go. That summer we saw and heard the whining of chain saws, the crash of tall trees, and the fleets of logging trucks roaring down the mountain roads with huge logs headed for the pulp mills. Big time logging arrived in the Oakland Hills. Frank Havens would have been delighted.

Today Roundtop is nearly denuded of eucalyptus. This does not mean, however, that the history of change has come to an end. Bay trees, toyons, Monterey pines, coyote bush, poison oak, and coffee berry that grew up in the shade of the eucalyptus have been left behind. Along with the newly arrived grasses and wildflowers, they form an unstable environment that has never existed before —— a California eucalyptus forest minus the eucalyptus.

What will happen to this environment? Perhaps the grasses will take over the hillside once again. Or perhaps if we wait five or ten years the brush will seize control of Roundtop as it has in large areas of nearby Tilden and Redwood. Or if we wait still longer the bay trees and toyons may grow strong enough to form the core of a mixed hardwood forest. There is also a chance that the Monterey pines will recover from injuries inflicted by the recent logging and will consolidate themselves into a dark pine forest that will cover parts of Roundtop. It is even possible that the eucalyptus will re-establish itself by sprouting from roots and stumps or from seeds that are now lying dormant in the ground. Frankly, I am not sure what is going to happen here. But I do know that for us plant watchers the next few decades at Roundtop are going to be among the most fascinating in its extraordinary history.

Sunol Wilderness

Many years ago, in the days when the Sunday drive was a major form of recreation, there existed a genteel ritual known as the "family picnic." Dad, mom, the kids, and some extra relatives (there were always extra relatives back then) would pack into the family buggy and sputter away to a park like Sunol. Here they spread their blankets along the shores of Alameda Creek. Like Spanish *conquistadors* they laid claim to the picnic tables and barbecue pits scattered along its banks. Small checkdams across the creek provided them with splash pools for swimming. Sunday artists set up their easels, kids swam and played ball, and grandfathers (dressed in Sunday suits and neckties) took off their shoes and let their liberated toes wiggle joyously in the cool grass. Here and there a stammering accordian could be heard. ("How well he plays, and he's only eleven!") The air smelled of hot dogs, pickles, and home-made pies. From the nearby woods blue jays, squirrels, and mice could scarcely contain their excitement as they watched the potato chips rain upon the ground like manna.

Today this genteel ritual is still being practiced at Sunol Regional Park —— complete with splash pools, picnic tables, barbecue pits, and big noisy families. In addition to family groups the picnic areas have also become popular with partying teenagers. But that makes it all the better for the squirrels, blue jays, and the mice.

"Ah," exclaim thousands of little animals. "More potato chips!"

Sunol is also a favorite with still another group: hikers who park their cars near the entrance and with a rucksack, an appropriate field guide, a map, binoculars, and a package of dried apricots head across the footbridge and away from the picnic areas. They follow miles of trails out into the wilds of Sunol, over the meadows, through the oak forests, up the mountains, and beyond to the distant ridges. They wander alongside the broad, rushing creek that gave Alameda County its name —— a creek which for many people is the most exciting feature of Sunol (see page 102). They hike out into this enormously spacious land where there are still eagles, falcons, mountain lions, bobtail cats, and coyotes —— out onto this big-hill, cow-dotted, almost Alpine wilderness where vastness comes in many forms.

The back-country of Sunol is mostly mountainous meadowland with open, sun-

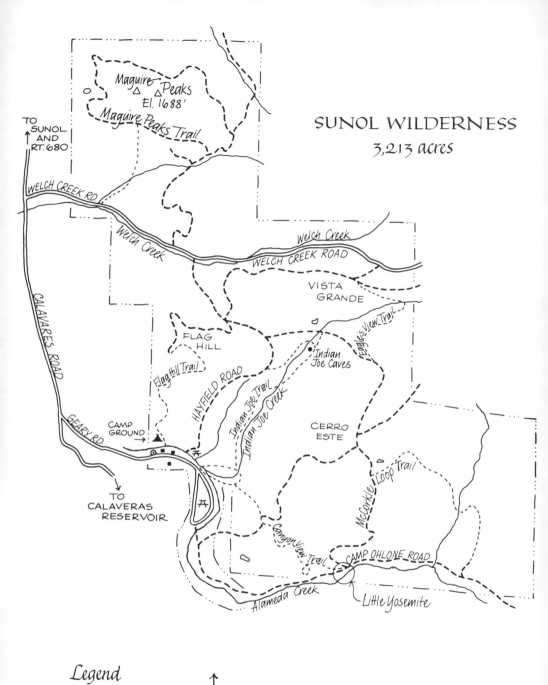

SUNOL WILDERNESS
3,213 acres

Maguire Peaks
El. 1688'

Maguire Peaks Trail

TO SUNOL AND RT. 680

WELCH CREEK RD.

Welch Creek

Welch Creek

WELCH CREEK ROAD

VISTA GRANDE

Eagle's View Trail

FLAG HILL

Flag Hill Trail

Indian Joe Caves

HAYFIELD ROAD

Indian Joe Trail

Indian Joe Creek

CERRO ESTE

CALAVARES ROAD

CAMP GROUND

GEARY RD.

TO CALAVERAS RESERVOIR

McCorkle Loop Trail

Canyon View Trail

CAMP OHLONE ROAD

Alameda Creek

Little Yosemite

Legend

PAVED ROAD.........
HIKING & RIDING.....
FOOTPATH...........
STREAM.............
PARK BOUNDARY....
PARK BUILDING........ ■
PARKING LOT.......... ⊙
PICNIC AREA.......... ⟨picnic symbol⟩

↑ N

scale of miles

0   ¼   ½   ¾   1

dappled forests of oak. Look closely at an oak some time, and you'll realize that it is more than just a tree. It is a bus —— a bus that carries many odd passengers on their journeys through life. Oak moth caterpillars build cobweb cities that cover the branches of some oak trees. There are lichen, mosses, and strange bugs in the furrows of the bark. Another kind of lichen droops like Spanish moss from the branches. Birds build nests, while galls and mistletoes live out their curious existences.

Galls (or "oak apples") hang in bunches from the trees. A gall is formed when a wasp stings the bark of the tree and lays its eggs. The oak reacts by manufacturing a thick coating around the eggs to isolate them, and this thick coating is what we call the gall. It protects the oak tree against the hatching wasps, but at the same time it also protects the hatching wasps against their enemies. Within the closed gall the eggs produce small, white, beanlike larvae. The larvae eat their way through the tissues of the gall until they approach the outer shell where they pause and spin a cocoon. Here young wasps are born, tunnel the rest of the way through the gall, and fly out into the wide mysterious world to repeat the mating and egg-laying process. Other insects now crawl into the empty gall looking for left-over food. And woodpeckers drill into the old galls looking for other insects.

As for mistletoes, these grow in big clumps near the tops of the trees. They look like the nests of some gigantic bird when seen from the distance. They bear a crop of white berries that are poisonous to people. But birds eat the berries enthusiastically. Within each berry is a sticky, indigestible seed which the birds often rub off their beaks onto the surface of the tree. Here the seed germinates. The roots probe deep into the host tree, fastening themselves onto the life system of the oak and stealing food and moisture directly from the tree's tissues. It is not, however, a complete parasite. Mistletoe does have chlorophyll, and it manufactures some of its own food.

To the druids of Britain the mistletoe was the "golden bough," the most sacred of all sacred plants. On the sixth night of the new moon a priest in white robes would climb the tree and cut down the mistletoe with a solid gold sickle. The plant was used for religious and medical rites. It was so valuable that the priests would sacrifice two white bulls to the gods in exchange for it. Of all the powerful rituals surrounding this plant, only a hint remains today: the quaint Christmas custom of kissing under the mistletoe.

To me the oak groves of Sunol with their light, airy mood and the strange life they support have a spiritual vastness to them that is very real, yet impossible to pin down.

Spend some time here underneath the oak trees. After all, Buddha found enlightenment under a banyan tree. Sir Isaac Newton discovered gravity under an apple tree. Who knows which of the hundreds of mysteries that still remain undiscovered will some day be revealed to some one sitting quietly underneath an oak tree?

Beyond the oak groves stretch the high meadowlands of Sunol. You can best explore these meadows by crossing them slowly, deliberately, and (please take me seriously) on all fours. Push your face into the grass and look really hard, until you find yourself totally immersed in the hidden world of sprouts, mouse tunnels, earthworm castings, gopher holes, and the epic journeys of bugs. You soon discover that all blades of grass are not alike. They may be thick or needle-thin, stiff or pliant, tall or short, whole or nibbled, smooth or fuzzy, and they come in dozens of different shades. If you focus all your attention on the ground, a clump of moss expands to the size of an Amazon rain jungle. Insects appear monstrous, fascinating, other-worldly. Dozens of tiny, insignificant flowers you never noticed before now burn before your eyes like furnaces roaring away on the meadow floor. A small patch of meadowland can become incredibly vast.

If you concentrate too hard on the grass beneath you, of course, a spring shower might suddenly catch you in the middle of a field. For goodness sakes, don't run for cover. Instead, get down on your belly so you won't miss a thing. A drop of rain falls, hits a blade of grass, and knocks it down. The raindrop then slides slowly off, and the grass, relieved of the weight, springs up again. As more drops fall, more blades of grass pop up and down until the whole field comes alive, wildly jitterbugging in the rain, and creating one of the merriest sights you've ever seen.

The intimacy to be gained with the meadows and oak groves is one of the major joys of Sunol. But there are times when this intimacy is overshadowed by the immensity of the park and the land around it. From the top of McGuire Peak, Eagle's View, Vista Grande, Flag Hill, and other places within the park you can look out over distant storm-tossed mountains and valleys. Sunol Regional Park itself is 3,500 acres; but all around it are huge expanses of wild land. It is this reservoir of wild land that fosters the existence of eagles and mountain lions in the East Bay, and which bestows on Sunol a true wilderness excitement.

Needless to say a wilderness in Alameda County is in constant jeopardy. I was

once hiking in Sunol when a jet plane whined overhead. Almost immediately a cat-bird hopped out of the brush to the top of a nearby tree and began to scold loudly at the plane, obviously protecting its territory. I understood the feeling. Those who love Sunol and the land around it have spent many years defending it against proposed quarries, guest ranches, and subdivisions. And the fight is far from won.

What future does this wilderness have? The East Bay Regional Park District has tentative plans to purchase 13,000 acres of private land around Sunol. In addition there has been talk that the adjacent lands of the San Francisco Water Company might be opened to the public on a "compatible use" basis. If these developments come to pass, we can look forward to a future in which Sunol Regional Park will be a wilderness area that approaches in scale and quality some of the State and even Federal wilderness areas —— the last wilderness remaining in this part of the Diablo Range.

Tilden

Tilden Park is a bus ride away from downtown Berkeley. It's hard to imagine: 2,065 acres of rolling grasslands, high hills, chaparral, lakes, forests, rivers, marshes, caves, and canyons practically in our back yards.

No matter what day of the week you visit Tilden it always seems to be Sunday afternoon. There is a permanent holiday spirit to this park. People wander along the hiking trails and over the hills, coming every day to walk their dogs, jog, or just stretch their minds —— the rustic equivalents of *boulevardiers* you find strolling about in a big city. Families picnic in the flowering meadows. Young Berkeley-ites with guitars head up the slopes. Some people get only as far as the creek bed a few feet from their picnic tables, while others have spent the whole day hiking deep into Wildcat Canyon or high into the hills.

Along the valley floor of Tilden the East Bay Regional Park District has con-centrated many "attractions." Personally, I prefer wild land to be left alone, but when my three year old son begins hounding me for "something special," as often as not we head for Tilden. And we both have a fine time.

For the kids there is an antique merry-go-round with hand-carved horses and an organ cranking out raunchy, spirited music —— music loaded with nostalgia and vitality. There are also pony rides and a miniature train pulled by a genuine steam locomotive. At the Little Farm goats, cows, sheep, donkeys, and more —— a full cast of farm animals —— loaf around a miniature barn. There is a staff of natural-ists at the Nature Area who talk about the spaghetti tree, the cough drop tree, and other bits of nonsense that make a lot of sense to kids. Previously their tours were limited to organized groups; but with the opening of the Environmental Education Center and museum in 1974, a broad range of naturalist activities is offered. Call 525-2233 for a schedule of events.

Other attractions of Tilden include Lake Anza (see page 71) where one can swim and Jewel Lake, a big duck pond with a self-guiding nature trail. There's also horse-back riding (private stables outside the park can rent you a horse), tennis courts, an archery range, an exhibit of old California farm machinery, an 18-hole golf course, dozens of picnic sites, and the Brazil Building which can be reserved for meetings or parties. At the Botanic Garden cactuses from the Mohave Desert rub shoulders with flowers from the coastal bluffs, pines from the High Sierras, and redwoods from the Oregon border. This diverse plant life has attracted a wide variety of birds who (like us) hop happily from one environment to the next without having to migrate.

In addition to the attractions Tilden has lots of land to explore. There are several different forests. There is the thick oak-bay forest of the canyons and the valleys. There are the Monterey pines which were planted here long ago. And there are extensive forests of eucalyptus —— as hard as marble and as straight as masts, their straightness emphasized by the recent freeze which killed the outermost branches. Each spring deer bring their wobbly, freshly licked fawns out of these forests to feed timidly on the fringes. Blue jays scold and complain —— ordinary jays, as exotic and striking as Aztec gods. Quail (plump matrons in fashionable plume hats) burst like firecrackers each spring into trails of scurrying chicks.

Outside the forests are the vast expanses of grassland and the patches of brush. After every rain dozens of little brooks come out of hiding to play upon the meadows. They dance, bounce, and twinkle as if trying to escape the clutches of their brainless

taskmaster, gravity. And we laugh along with the brooks, because we know that no matter how hard gravity tries the brooks will be born again, again, and still again with each succeeding rain.

Tilden Park was originally called Wildcat Canyon. It was renamed after Charles Lee Tilden, the first president of the Park District's Board of Directors. The board meetings often took place in Tilden's home, and in these early years he even loaned the District money out of his pocket to cover expenses.

The land has had a varied history. Costanoan Indians had a village here, and arrowheads and other artifacts still turn up occasionally. The next settlers were herds of cattle from the Mission Dolores in San Francisco, who roamed freely over the hills. Then came the Spaniards, and later the Anglos. There was once a quarry and a slaughterhouse here. W. P. A. crews of the Depression built many of the roads, buildings, and trails, as well as the golf course. During the Second World War over 2,000 soldiers were stationed here, and throughout the eucalyptus forests you can still find remains of the foxholes they dug.

Tilden, in other words, is hardly a wilderness. Much of the land has been given over to artificial lakes, irrigated lawns, a golf course, groves of exotic trees, dozens of attractions, and the paved roads that crisscross the park. Yet despite all these things, the park projects a big, generous mood of its own. It reminds me of a favorite uncle who spends the afternoon down on his hands and knees while we little kids pull and jump, play "horsey", and scamper over his back. At the end of the day the uncle gets up, brushing away all the little kids, a bit tired, a little sore, but still as big and mellow as ever.

For hundreds of years different cultures, events, and attractions have scampered over the back and shoulders of Tilden. The park, of course, shows the signs of everything we have done to it. But beneath these signs we feel the influence of a mellow piece of land that seems bigger than anything that has happened to it. Spiritually, Tilden has remained unchanged. This is still a place where we, like the Indians before us, can feel the wind, hear the trees creak, smell the earth, lie down in soft grass, and let our minds bounce laughingly after butterflies.

Or we can climb up the backs of the broad meadows to the top of Wildcat Peak. Here on a clear day we can look way beyond the cities that fringe the Bay, through the Golden Gate into the Pacific, up into the mouth of the Sacramento, over hundreds of square miles of meadows, forests, lakes, and reservoirs, sometimes as far as the snowcapped peaks in the distance. Tilden is part of this grand scenery. There is a wildness, freedom, and spaciousness to these hills, and for many of us who live in cities it has helped keep alive a wildness and spaciousness within us.

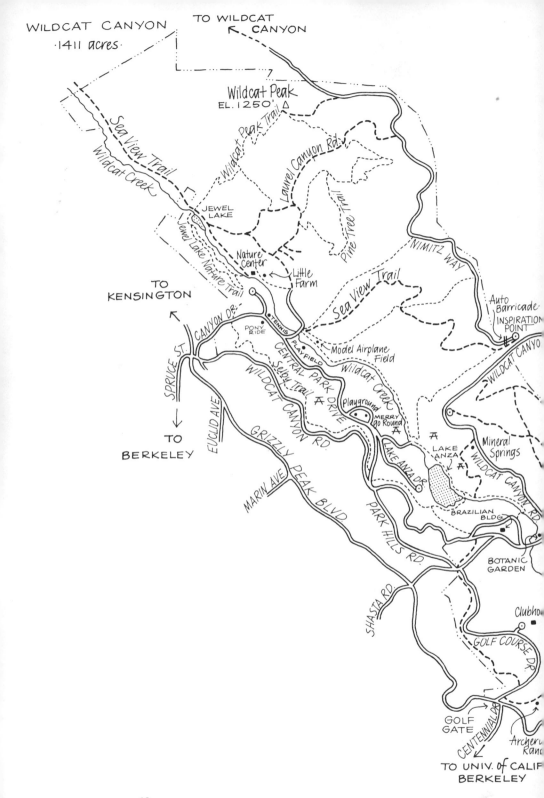

WILDCAT CANYON
·1411 acres·

TO WILDCAT CANYON

Wildcat Peak
EL. 1250'

Sea View Trail
Wildcat Creek

Wildcat Peak Trail

Laurel Canyon Rd.

Pine Tree Trail

JEWEL LAKE

Jewel Lake Nature Trail

NIMITZ WAY

Sea View Trail

Nature Center

Little Farm

TO KENSINGTON

SPRUCE ST.

CANYON DR.

PONY RIDE

TENNIS

PLAYFIELD

Model Airplane Field

CENTRAL PARK DRIVE

Selby Trail

Wildcat Creek

Auto Barricade
INSPIRATION POINT

WILDCAT CANYON

TO BERKELEY

EUCLID AVE.

WILDCAT CANYON RD.

Playground

MERRY go Round

LAKE ANZA DR.

LAKE ANZA

Mineral Springs

WILDCAT CANYON RD.

GRIZZLY PEAK BLVD.

MARIN AVE.

BRAZILIAN BLDG

PARK HILLS RD.

BOTANIC GARDEN

SHASTA RD.

Clubho

GOLF COURSE DR.

GOLF GATE

CENTENNIAL DR.

Archery Rang

TO UNIV. of CALIF
BERKELEY

48

TILDEN

2,065 acres

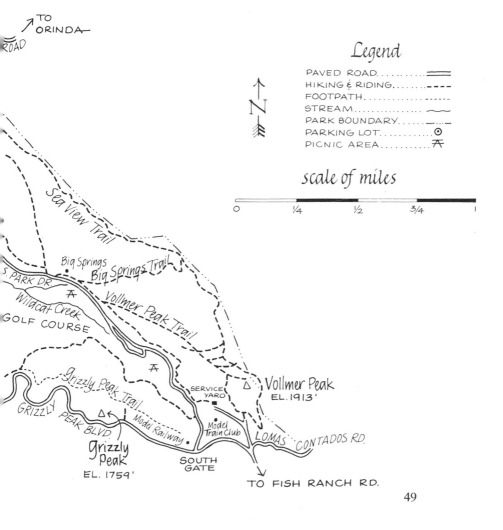

TO ORINDA

ROAD

Sea View Trail

Big Springs

Big Springs Trail

S. PARK DR.

Wildcat Creek

Vollmer Peak Trail

GOLF COURSE

Grizzly Peak Trail

GRIZZLY PEAK BLVD.

Model Railway

SERVICE YARD

Model Train Club

Vollmer Peak
EL. 1913'

LOMAS CONTADOS RD.

Grizzly Peak
EL. 1759'

SOUTH GATE

TO FISH RANCH RD.

49

Las Trampas Wilderness

Las Trampas is about 2,500 acres of wilderness. Golden eagles are regularly sighted here, hunting smoothly and silently over the meadows. They survey the land with wise disdainful eyes, perhaps unaware that there are no longer Indians in these valleys to collect their feathers and worship them as gods. The worshippers have long since disappeared, and the eagles now look down upon flocks of bluebirds with their pink-tinged breasts and cheerful dispositions, bouncing lightly among the flowers and grazing cows. I often think of Las Trampas as an eagle-bluebird wilderness. Its rugged terrain and rich wildlife might inspire awe elsewhere, but in the wombs of these benevolent valleys "awe" becomes a gentle, laughing sense of wonderment.

The wildlife in Las Trampas is unbelievably rich. Mountain lions prowl the ridges, tending their cautious herds of deer. Red foxes, gray foxes, bobcats, ringtails, raccoons, skunks, coyotes, and weasels —— shy and reluctant animals —— hunt throughout the valleys and canyons. Yet despite the best efforts of these skillful hunters squirrels, mice, and rabbits lead fat, bold, and prosperous lives. To support this rich and varied wildlife, many different environments come together at Las Trampas. There are delightful woodlands sprinkled with meadows —— meadows like flowering bowls brimming over with bird songs. Northwest of Eagle's Peak in the recently acquired Corduroy Hills area is a big forested canyon, as nearly unexplored as any area in the East Bay. The south facing (sun facing) slopes of Las Trampas Ridge support a spicy smelling elfin forest of chaparral bushes. Sycamores and bay trees shade the creeks, while most of the slope that leads up to Rocky Ridge is a vast treeless meadow of grasses and spring wildflowers. And everywhere are huge slabs of rock, tossed and crumpled, fragmented and compacted, uplifted and worn down again by millions of years of geological indecision and revolt.

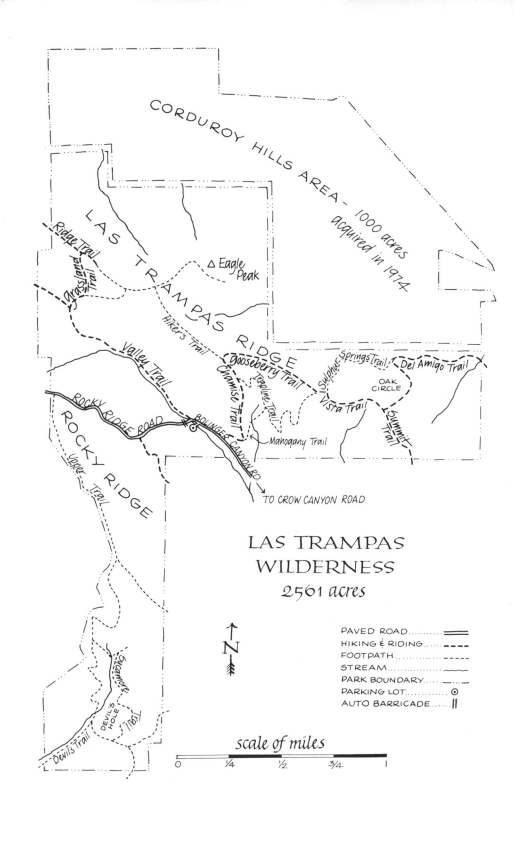

CORDUROY HILLS AREA - 1000 acres
acquired in 1974

LAS TRAMPAS RIDGE

Ridge Trail

Grassland Trail

△ Eagle Peak

Hiker's Trail

Valley Trail

Gooseberry Trail

Chamise Trail

Trapline Trail

Sulphur Springs Trail

Del Amigo Trail

OAK CIRCLE

Vista Trail

Summit Trail

ROCKY RIDGE ROAD

BOLINGER CANYON RD

Mahogany Trail

ROCKY RIDGE

Upper Trail

TO CROW CANYON ROAD

LAS TRAMPAS
WILDERNESS
2561 acres

Sycamore Trail

DEVIL'S HOLE Trail

Devil's Trail

N

PAVED ROAD .... ▬▬▬
HIKING & RIDING .... ▬ ▬ ▬
FOOTPATH ....
STREAM ....
PARK BOUNDARY ...... ▬ · ▬
PARKING LOT .... ⊙
AUTO BARRICADE ...... ‖

scale of miles

0   ¼   ½   ¾   1

These many environments create niches for many rare animals, birds, and **plants**. But rarest of all, the very richness of the park gets us to re-examine the so-called *ordinary* world around us. It was here, for example, that I discovered the wind. We usually take the wind for granted. But Rocky Ridge rises 2,000 feet above sea level, and it has some of the most extraordinary wind that can be found in the Bay Area.

Wind does not just blow mechanically, like the current of dull, stupid air produced by an electric fan. It has infinite variety. Most of the time it is light and whimsical. It slaps you playfully on the cheek, it tickles you lovingly near the ear. One gust is warm and languid, another cool, sharp, and clear. One minute it blows with the determination of a grand opera, and then it trails off forgetfully into nothing. Even the most savage, biting wind pauses now and then in its howling for a moment of lyrical refreshment. As you reach the ridgetop you might sit down somewhere, close your eyes, and give yourself over to the wind. It can leave you as refreshed as if you had just stepped out of the hands of a master masseur.

How does the landscape react to thousands and thousands of years of wind? Along Rocky Ridge you will find a large stone outcropping that is pockmarked with caves. These caves are sculptures of the wind. Look inside them for a view of many miniature Bryce Canyons with their sandstone swirls, circular gouges, archways, tunnels, and cornucopias —— the strangely soothing, whimsical calligraphy of the wind.

I've spent many days hiking through Las Trampas, and I've found it to be a remote, primitive experience. The one exception is the hike along Rocky Ridge Road, a paved road that bisects the park and leads to a military installation beyond the park's boundaries. But in the springtime all sorts of unusual bugs (the unsung wildlife of Las Trampas) come tumbling out of the grasslands onto the pavement. I remember once watching a woman push a stroller up the road. She stooped down to examine a spider which was covered with dozens of baby spiders wriggling on her back. The spider seemed to shock the woman. And the woman most certainly shocked the spider which scurried across the road. Yet I wonder whether either party realized that they were both engaged in exactly the same act: transporting their babies across Rocky Ridge Road.

But Rocky Ridge Road is untypical of Las Trampas's trails. Most of them are delightfully narrow, unsophisticated foot trails that bring you close to the wildlife and lead you unobtrusively through the forests and meadows up to the ridgetops. They are trails where you can become intimate with your immediate surroundings while gazing out across vast panoramas.

Both of the ridgetops in this park (Las Trampas Ridge and Rocky Ridge) are prominent landmarks in the Bay Area, and each provides an utterly spectacular view. From Las Trampas Ridge you can look out over the San Ramon Valley, where Mount Diablo looms up close, like a huge mother hen clucking and brooding over her flock of little chick hills. From Rocky Ridge you can see the vast parallel ridges of the Coast Range extending toward the Bay and southward. I am always heartened by this view of so many square miles of still wild, undeveloped land remaining in the East Bay.

From these ridgetops there is, however, an even more distant, mind-expanding view. You can find it by looking, not out to the horizon, but down at your feet. Examine the rocks on the ridgetops, and you are likely to find the remains of clamshells embedded in them —— sure evidence that these towering ridges were once under water. In fact at various times this area was an ocean dotted with islands. Fossils found in and around Las Trampas also show that this area once consisted of plains and marshes where mastodons and camels grazed alongside other equally improbable animals. In still more distant times the charming meadows and forests you can see from the ridgetops were a stark landscape of hissing volcanos.

The saga of geological change is one of the truly grand and heroic tales that modern science has given us. Forces within the earth have thrust up immense mountain chains, and these mountain chains have time and again been worn back to the sea. What are the mighty forces that wear down mountains? Look around you and you can see them at work.

Aside from the wind with its delicate sculpturings, a second powerful force of erosion is water. One of the best water shows takes place in Devil's Hole, a box canyon on the other side of Rocky Ridge. This is an area of massive stone walls and rugged slopes. For several days after a rainstorm water seeps out through cracks on the stony ledges, flows in sheets down the rock faces, and gathers itself into a splashing, cascading, laughing little creek. Some day I hope you'll stop at the creek and spend a half hour or so playing with the water, running it through your fingers, looking at its formlessness (it takes its shape "negatively," from whatever solids contain it), feeling its coolness, and watching all its delightful tricks. Water is so common that we take it for granted, just as we tend to take the whole miracle of being alive for granted.

But look at water freshly some time. Pretend that you are a spaceman who has just arrived on earth. You find a clear pool in the creek. It looks hard and flat, like a big metallic jewel. You step into it and it shatters. Heartbroken, you withdraw your foot, but the jewel reforms itself as perfect as before. You bring out a magnifier, but you cannot find any sign of where the water was broken. The more you study the pool the stranger it gets. It reflects light, yet you can see through it. It's colorless, yet plainly visible. You try to pick some up, but it slips through your fingers. The longer you play with it the more oddities you discover, until you are certain that you have just happened upon the most incredible substance in the whole

universe —— which may very well be true.

A third erosive force on these ridges is lichen. Lichen looks like splotches and crusts on the rocks, but it is really a primitive plant. It exudes an acid that imperceptibly breaks down the rocks, turning them into soil that will sustain plants —— until eventually the soil is washed downhill by the water.

Lichen, wind, and water do not work by brute force. They work slowly, patiently, and over many millions of years. But they never give up. How long will it take them to grind these ridges down to sea level again? Think about this the next time you are in Las Trampas and you will get some idea of the vast stretches of time over which geological changes take place. Lichen, wind, water, and embedded clamshells, if you think deeply about them, will open up like doors through which you can step from Las Trampas into another consciousness —— the immense consciousness of geological time.*

For more information about the geology, wildlife, and botany of Las Trampas, get a copy of The Story of Las Trampas by Walter Knight. This book contains checklists and many casual and scientific observations. It costs $2.50 (plus 25¢ postage), and it can be ordered through the East Bay Regional Park District.

Bay

The San Francisco Bay has always been one of the best kept secrets in the State. Juan Cabrillo was the first European to explore the California coast in 1543, and he missed the Golden Gate completely, sailing right past the one narrow opening to the Bay. For the next 226 years explorers, merchantmen, and pirates plied the coast without ever guessing the presence of this vast body of water. It remained hidden until 1769 when Gaspar de Portola, marching northward from Monterey with more important things on his mind, stumbled upon it accidentally.

Despite Portola, the Bay is still largely undiscovered. We are the modern day explorers, merchantmen, and pirates as we speed by it on freeways, speed over it on bridges, and speed under it on **BART** trains. We catch glimpses of it between factories. But over 260 of its 275 miles of shoreline are off limits to the public. Sadly, the Bay has become like a movie star or a great public figure: every one knows about it and talks about it, but very few are really intimate with it.

Yet (despite all we have done to it) the Bay is still alive and kicking, teeming with wildlife, as free and wild as the cries of its seagulls. You can rediscover the Bay by walking along its beaches, tramping through its marshes, or sitting quietly under its sea bluffs at these three East Bay Regional Parks: Alameda Beach, Coyote Hills, and Point Pinole.

Alameda Beach

Alameda Beach is a skinny stretch of sand and rock that runs two and a half miles along the Bay at Alameda. There is swimming, sun-bathing, shell collecting, and bird watching here. Hundreds of people come to fly kites in the spring winds. Professional athletes run through the sand to build muscles —— and in case you've forgotten, nothing builds muscles quite like running through the sand.

Looking at things uncharitably, Alameda Beach has a shoddy, down-in-the-mouth appearance that urban beaches often have. Housing developments run down to the borders of the beach. Jets roar overhead. Plastic spoons and scrap wood dumped into the Bay at other places float onto the shore and must be cleaned up. Alameda Beach is very much part of the Bay Area. It has all the noise and pollution which we all know very well. But it also has a lot of the beauty and drama of the Bay which we too often ignore. There is tide and wind and the sun. There's a big sense of time that you get from spending a day at the beach, and a big sense of scale that you feel from looking across the Bay to the hazy mountains in the distance. Alameda Beach is a good place to get in touch with the rhythms of the Bay —— or perhaps even the rhythms of your own consciousness.

You'd never guess it at first glance, but Alameda Beach is rich in wildlife. The wildlife is mostly underground. It consists of clams, oysters, many kinds of worms, barnacles, shrimps, crabs, creatures that burrow in the sand, and creatures that cling to rocks. Want to get acquainted with this wildlife? Join the Underground! If you think human beings have strange habits, just consider. At Alameda Beach there are oysters that change sex every year (male one year, female the next). There are flatworms that can digest their internal organs in times of starvation and grow new ones later on. Alameda Beach has many incredible forms of life which you can see, study, and handle. There are strange, marvelous happenings in the mud and under the rocks. Lift a rock and see what scurries out. Bring a magnifying glass to study and contemplate these exotic little animals. But afterwards, as an act of ecological courtesy, please replace the rocks in their original positions to keep these creatures' environments intact.

At the southern end of the park is a cordgrass marsh that is set aside as a bird sanctuary. Cordgrass is a super-grass that thrives in salty soil and is actually five times as nutritious as wheat. In fact it is considered to be the most productive type of natural vegetation in North America. When the grass dies and decays, tons of nutrients are released. And the ooze of a cordgrass marsh is like a Thanksgiving feast that attracts an unbelievable concentration of mollusks, crustaceans, and smaller forms of life. This in turn is what attracts all those thousands of birds you find here, delicately sliding their long bills into the mud.

If you want to learn more about the environments at Alameda Beach, call 525-2233 and ask about the scheduled naturalist talks. These talks are generally available only to schools and youth groups, but there are open house dates when every one is invited free.

Every year Alameda Beach holds a sand castle contest. Kids build sand castles, sand palaces, sand fortresses, and sand cathedrals on the beach. Every year exquisite sand civilizations rise up and flourish briefly until the next high tide.

This reminds me of the history of Alameda Beach.

The first great sand civilization that arose here was that of the Indians who collected oysters and clams along the Bay shore. Only the shell mounds further inland are left to remind us of the Indian civilization that was once here.

Then came Neptune Beach which flourished briefly between 1890 and 1939. Neptune Beach was built to rival Copenhagen's Tivoli Gardens. It had a ballroom, swimming pool, skating rink, and theater. The years added a roller coaster, merry-go-round, thrill rides, and honky-tonk, as Neptune Beach became the "Coney Island of the West." Edwin Booth acted here, boxers "Gentleman Jim" Corbett and Bob Fitzsimmons trained here, and Robert Louis Stevenson and Jack London wrote here. But by 1939 the automobile, the Bay Bridge, other amusement parks, and changing tastes drove Neptune Beach into bankruptcy. By now nearly all traces have been obliterated.

The next great sand civilization was the U. S. Maritime Training Center built during the Second World War. The seamen are gone now, but the East Bay Regional Park District still uses the hospital as its naturalists' headquarters and the boat-shaped *Glory of the Sea* training center as a maintenance garage.

Then came the developers who in the early 1950's began to fill the land between the Alameda Lagoon and the present beach. They pumped sand from the bottom of the Bay to fill out the current contours of Alameda Beach.

In 1967 the State of California and the City of Alameda leased the beach to the East Bay Regional Park District. The Park District is the present sand civilization. It has added a bath house, snack bar, and picnic areas. It has planted green lawns, built a day camp shelter, is nursing along some still puny shade trees, and has assigned a crew to keep the beach clean. Naturally, the East Bay Regional Park District thinks that its hold on Alameda Beach is permanent. So did the other sand civilizations. Today the Bay is beating up against the beach, trying to reclaim the filled in portions, nibbling at the shorelines, trying relentlessly to gobble up Alameda Beach once more. You can see the signs of the battle all along the beach. The latest sand civilization, however, has undertaken engineering studies and insists it will persevere —— if not forever, perhaps for the rest of this geological age. Perhaps.

Coyote Hills

Coyote Hills Regional Park is a 1,000 acre park along the bayshore near Newark. The Hills themselves are a Lilliputian mountain range, rising only 200 to 300 feet high, and surrounded by flatness. Not uniformity, mind you, but flatness —— an amazing patchwork of flat environments all teeming with wildlife. To the west of the Hills are saltwater marshes, mudflats, the neatly framed salt evaporating ponds, and (in the distance) the wide expanse of the Bay. To the east of the Hills are freshwater marshes, grassy meadows, horse pastures, and well beyond the park's boundaries the vegetable farms and broad plains of Newark, Fremont, and Union City. The only high spots between here and the Hayward Hills are the flood control levees that chaperone Alameda Creek along the northern borders of the park, and three slight humps in the marshy area near the park's eastern border. These humps are no more than about fifteen feet high, but they have received a lot of attention in recent years. They are the only visible remains of an Indian civilization that flourished from about 2,000 B. C. until the turn of the present century.

This flat countryside is largely the creation of Alameda Creek. In fact Coyote Hills were once islands in the middle of the Bay —— very similar geologically to Angel Island. Every year for thousands of years Alameda Creek brought down its tons of silt from the mountains and deposited it around the islands to create this low marshy land. The Hills still have the feeling of islands, but they are islands in the middle of a marshland.

The saltwater ponds and marshes, the freshwater marshes, and the hillside meadows combine to make Coyote Hills a three-ring circus of bird life. The saltwater marshes are probably the richest wildlife environment in North America, and a few patches of untouched marshland remain. But most of them have been diked and flooded to form the salt evaporating ponds of Leslie Salt Company. While the ponds are not quite as hospitable to bird life as the marshes, they still attract legions of gulls, terns, avocets, and stilts who feed on brine shrimp and on the other creatures of these warm shallow waters. Sandpipers race like skittlebugs over the mudflats, while egrets and herons tiptoe through the water like aristocrats who find it slightly distasteful to get their feet wet.

On the grasslands and hillsides phoebes, swallows, shrikes, and flocks of well-tailored meadow larks harvest the fringes of the vast insect population. Red-tailed hawks sweep low over the hills and meadows, caressing the land's contours like fortune tellers passing their hands over a crystal ball. They are looking for ground squirrels, gophers, snakes, mice, or jack rabbits that thrive in the tall grass.

In the freshwater marshes blackbirds, red-winged blackbirds, and the uncommon tri-colored blackbirds all flock and bustle. Overhead fly the rare white-tailed kites and marsh hawks. Life is incredibly abundant. You can sit alongside the water and watch the mosquito larvae swim with snorkle tubes, or diving beetles who take bubbles of air with them into stagnant water —— the Jacques Cousteaus of the insect world. Frogs croak with obvious satisfaction, "Ten-eight, ten-eight, ten-eight."

Muskrats play a very important part in the marsh ecology. If it weren't for them these shallow waters would quickly choke up with cattails and tules. Fortunately, the muskrats have a good appetite for roots. They keep the ponds and the passageways clear, and their dens rise like pyramids in the patches of blue water.

But in the late fall the most spectacular show of them all begins, as the marshes swell with the first rains and the massive flocks of ducks arrive from Alaska and Canada. Some flocks are so large you can hear the whirring of their wings as they fly overhead. These are not tame ducks you can bribe with a piece of stale bread. They are wild ducks, wary of hunters and worldly-wise. You can't get too close, so bring binoculars and sit back somewhere to enjoy the Greatest Duck Show in the Bay. There are ducks who sit high in the water, princely ducks moving effortlessly like maharajas being carried on sedan chairs. And then there are those who sit low in the water and seem to be fighting, kicking, and pumping hard just to make a few inches. Diving ducks slip easily beneath the water, scarcely rippling the surface as they disappear from sight. While the dabblers thrust only their necks and heads under water, leaving their ecstatic behinds wiggling and waggling in the air. In the spring the great flocks become restless and head north again, leaving behind them a smaller number of resident ducks to nest and raise their young in the shrink-

ing waters of the marsh.

The rich environments of Coyote Hills were ideal for the Indians who once lived here. Their houses looked like upside-down bowls, framed with bent willows, thatched with tules, and covered with thick layers of mud. The people were one of the many sub-tribes of the Costanoans, and although they lived on this spot until the turn of the present century, very little is known about them. Many times, though, I find myself envying their diet: abalone, oysters, clams, mussels, and snails from the unpolluted Bay; salmon, sturgeon, and trout from the un-channelized creek; birds' eggs from the willow thickets; rabbits, squirrels, deer, elk, seals, and antelope that they hunted or snared; plus berries, nuts, roots, a-corns, and the many seeds that went into making pinole. The Indians were so at home here, that after nearly 4,000 years of continuous habitation their only impact on the land has been three insignificant mounds of discarded shells and bones.

Today these mounds are fenced off as archaeological sites. I wish the archae-ologists well. But I also find it pathetic that we have crushed this civilization so totally that some of the best educated minds in the country are now crawling through their garbage and their graves to retrieve beads, broken needles, and fragments of mortars and pestles. We can measure their skulls right down to the most precise fraction of a millimeter, but there is no way we can ever learn the language they spoke, the songs they sang, the stories they told, their customs, crafts, dances, or the range of their emotions. Yet as little as the mounds can tell us, we are lucky to have even this much: of the 425 shell mounds recorded around the Bay in 1900, almost all the rest have disappeared beneath freeways, factories, tract homes, or into the maws of cement plants.

Which brings us to one of the prime mysteries of all: how in the world did this fine piece of Bayshore real estate avoid the usual fate of development? Coy-ote Hills was owned by a single family, the Pattersons, from 1852 until 1968 when it was taken over by the East Bay Regional Park District. A narrow gauge train plying the Newark-San Jose route once ran nearby, and as its whistles wailed across the plains coyotes living in these hills would howl in reply, thus giving the hills their name. But the coyotes were exterminated, and the area became the scene of an exclusive duck hunting club formed by Patterson along with members of the Bohemian Club. The land was stocked with pheasants, and even today as you hike through the brush and thickets you occasionally flush out one of these glowing, handsome birds.

By the 1950's the threat of development became very acute. The land was seriously considered by the U. S. Atomic Energy Commission as the site of Stanford University's two-mile long linear accelerator. In 1959 the Army moved onto the Patterson's property and erected a Nike missile base. Later the buildings from the Nike site were leased to the Biological Sonar Laboratory of the Stanford University Research Institute, and until 1974 they were the scene of experiments on the hearing abilities of seals and sea lions.

Since 1968 Coyote Hills has belonged to the East Bay Regional Park District. The flatness of the land has made it very popular with bicyclists, and you can rent a ten-speed or a three-speed bike at the park. There is also a staff of naturalists on hand who can answer such questions as: "What is the red glass-like rock that protrudes from the hilltops?"; or, "How do the salt evaporating ponds work?"; or, "Why is it so windy here?" The naturalists also often give public tours of the marshes, the shell mounds, and other features of the park. Call 471-4967 for more information.

What future does this varied but fragile environment have in the midst of a rapidly developing Bay Area? We have every reason to be optimistic. In addition to the protection offered by the East Bay Regional Park District, Coyote Hills now falls within the boundaries of the San Francisco Bay National Wildlife Refuge —— a recently formed refuge that covers 23,000 acres of salt ponds, marshes, and mudflats in the southern part of the Bay.

Point Pinole

"You've never been to Point Pinole?" my friend Dave once asked, looking at me as if I was some sort of cretin.

"You've been to Paris, but you've never been to Point Pinole? Go! Right now! You simply can't live another day without seeing Point Pinole."

I did get to Point Pinole (the first time was in 1971). I jumped the fence and evaded the guard hired by Bethlehem Steel who then owned the property. I felt totally bewildered —— like Alice must have felt when she slipped down the rabbit hole into a whole new world. Here, in Richmond California, one of the most highly developed industrial areas of the world, I found: three and a half miles of nearly virgin shoreline; over one square mile of rolling meadows; rare salt water marshes with almost extinct  birds; spectacular views across the Bay to Mount Tamalpais and the Marin coast; and, most welcome of all, a sense of spaciousness, depth, and tranquility I've gotten nowhere else in the Bay.

Visiting Point Pinole was like stepping into a mirage.

It still is like stepping into a mirage, except today you no longer have to jump the fence or play hide-and-seek with the Bethlehem Steel guards. Thanks to the urgings of conservations groups, the East Bay Regional Park District has bought Point Pinole, and the Point is now ours! As my friend Dave said, "You simply can't live another day without seeing Point Pinole."

In the springtime the spacious meadows come alive with greens, flowers, brooks, and meadow creatures. I once came upon what I thought was an invasion of grasshoppers; it turned out to be toads, millions (billions?) of tiny colorful toads hopping crazily over the meadows like dust motes in the sun.

Another time I was staring at a flower when to my amazement I saw a whole gallery of owl's heads staring back at me from among the petals. I had come upon owl's clover, one of the most plentiful wildflowers which grow on Point Pinole. And everywhere on the Point are the groves of weeping eucalyptus trees, housing some of the biggest, most impressive hawks in the Bay Area.

Birdwatchers consider Point Pinole one of the best places in the Bay for shore birds. If you want to get in on the action, come in the morning at low tide. (During the afternoon the setting sun creates a glare on the Bay that makes birdwatching difficult.) Bring your binoculars, park your car at the small parking lot above the playground next to Parchester Village, and climb across the railroad embankment. If the tide is low you will probably see more birds than you ever thought existed.

If you are a nouveau-birdwatcher, you may find the following guide somewhat helpful:

...If the bird is sitting on a piling sunning itself and looking wise, it is probably a cormorant.

...If the bird looks too delicate, like a tissue paper origami creation, it's probably a heron.

...If the bird looks like a duck and it dives deep for its food, it's probably a canvasback, grebe, loon, or scaup.

...If the bird is a duck and paddles around the shallows dipping for its food, it's probably a mallard, scoter, teal, or pinhead.

...If the bird is wandering over the shore intensely studying the ground as if it lost something important in the mud, it's probably a sandpiper, avocet, stilt, or a marbled godwit.

...If the bird flushes out of the pickleweed-cordgrass swamp, look sharp! You may have chanced upon an extremely rare California Clapper Rail or a Salt Marsh Song Sparrow.

You can watch birds, have picnics, fish, fly kites, or do almost anything you want at Point Pinole, but most people end up just wandering around. You can follow the shoreline for miles, alongside grassy meadows that roll gently down to the beach, or under sea bluffs that tower fifty feet above your head. This shoreline collects some of the most fascinating litter in the Bay Area. Pieces of wood, metal, fixtures, plastic spoons, and other familiar objects of civilization emerge from the Bay warped, corroded, encrusted with barnacles and invaded by seaweed. An ordinary tin can becomes transformed by the Bay into a grotesque piece of sculpture.

Along with manmade objects you also find seashells, crabs, seaweed, the body of a shark, or the delicate skeleton head of a heron. This flotsam is like the leftovers of a rich man's banquet: only a hint of the wealth of the Bay and a sign (halleluja) that despite all we have done, the Bay is still alive, alive, alive, and kicking.

People who come to Point Pinole usually leave with a sense of awe, a feeling of peacefulness, and a lot of unanswered questions. What are the peculiar bumps, humps, dips, and pits that are scattered throughout the meadows? What was the long pier near the tip of the Point used for? Why did this land stay so unspoiled, right in the middle of Richmond? How did it escape the fate that befell almost every other piece of Bayshore land in the East Bay?

Since the Civil War, Point Pinole has been used for the manufacture of gun powder. In the late 1890's Giant Powder Company (later Atlas Powder Company) began making dynamite and then nitro-glycerine here. To guard against the "big bang," the manufacturing process was carried on —— not all under one roof as in ordinary factories —— but in dozens of little buildings half buried in the ground and spread out over a huge area.

The precautions were extraordinary. There were several full-time safety specialists, and their word was law. Employees were searched at the gate to make sure they carried no matches. They could wear no metal, not even belt buckles or nails in their shoes, since metal might strike a spark. A narrow gauge train that serviced the buildings was powered by batteries. The pushcart that actually entered the buildings ran on hardwood rails rather than metal rails. Each day only as much explosives were manufactured as were needed to fill immediate orders. They were packed into aluminum crates. The crates were dipped into paraffin to seal them tight and were then brought to the pier. At the end of the day barges took the entire day's production out to waiting ships, and Point Pinole closed down for the night.

For about 100 years a high fence surrounded Point Pinole to keep out vandals, wanderers, and cigar smokers. As an accidental by-product it also kept out automobiles, factories, supermarkets, and housing developments.

"Why choose the most beautiful place in the whole Bay for a munitions factory?" I used to wonder. I wondered about that for a long time, in fact, until one day the massive truth dawned on me. That in the mid-19th century the whole Bayshore was as open and beautiful as Point Pinole. Point Pinole is different from downtown Oakland, downtown San Leandro, or downtown Richmond in only one respect: because of its curious history it has been left pretty much alone.

The explosives industry boomed (so to speak) until 1947, when a freakish accident in the Gulf of Mexico signalled the end. A shipload of ammonium nitrate fertilizer exploded, wiping out Texas City, Texas, killing or injuring over 3,000 people, and rattling buildings 160 miles away. If cheap fertilizer packed such a wallop, reasoned many people, why use expensive nitro-glycerine? And over the next decade ammonium nitrate came to replace the more traditional explosives.

In the early 1960's Atlas Powder Company closed down its Point Pinole operations and sold the land to Bethlehem Steel. Bethlehem planned to use all this vast acreage to build the world's largest steel mill and export steel to the Far East. But by the late 1960's Japan had developed a strong steel industry of its own, and Bethlehem Steel no longer needed all the land it had purchased.

For the next several years the destiny of Point Pinole hung in the air. Many Richmond officials wanted the Point industrialized or subdivided ——— "to keep it on the tax rolls." But conservationists launched an impressive, even passionate *Save Point Pinole* campaign. Finally, in 1972, Bethlehem Steel agreed to sell 1,000 acres of Point Pinole to the East Bay Regional Park District. Today Point Pinole is in the domain of picnickers, beachcombers, and weekend fishermen who have been bringing in excellent catches of flounder, sturgeon, and striped bass.

With the return of fishing the history of Point Pinole has come full circle. The Huchuin Indians had a permanent encampment in what is now San Pablo, and they too used to visit the Point frequently to fish. Then in 1772 Pedro Fages led a small company of soldiers into the area. The Europeans were tired and hungry, and the local Huchuins brought them a nourishing porridge made of acorn flour, seeds, and the grains of wild grasses. The Indians called this porridge *pinole,* and the grateful explorers gave this name to the whole area.

Today we are all explorers. Many of us are disillusioned and puzzled by the civilization we've created, and we too are setting out to find wild places. Point Pinole is one of the best of these wild places, and I think that it will be as hospitable to you as it was to the Spanish explorers almost exactly 200 years ago.

Lakes

There were once twenty-one creeks that flowed down from the Oakland-Berkeley Hills into the Bay. Packrat saw these creeks and to him they looked like bright silver ribbons. He wanted them something awful, and he stole them. With his friend the beaver he channelized, boxed, dammed, and culverted them out of existence. He stole them away so cleverly that today most of us city folks would never guess that a few blocks from our houses once ran a living creek.

But as we are coming to realize, this was a melancholy theft. Years ago when the thievery was still in the planning stage, we should have listened more lovingly to the babble of our creeks instead of the babble of highway and construction engineers. We'd be happier people if tree-lined creeks still flowed past our homes and meandered in and out of our daily thoughts. I might say to my neighbor (after commenting on the weather): "The water level is dropping in the creek, the neighborhood swimming holes will soon dry up, and the buckeyes will lose their leaves." These creeks were like lifelines that connected our cities to the hills, the rains, and the rhythms of nature. When packrat stole the lifelines he left us even more stranded and cut off than we were before.

The creeks no longer flow through our cities —— at least not as living creeks —— but the waters have not disappeared. The waters are waiting for us in the hills, big calm bodies of water standing patiently behind their dams, willing to give comfort and pleasure to any one who comes looking. Packrat stole the creeks, but in exchange he left us several artificial lakes.

Some of my friends have a kind of snobbishness toward these lakes, as if they owed it to the environment to hate artificial lakes. These lakes are all too recent, they feel. None of them existed in the days of the Indians or even the Spanish. They don't belong. They're newcomers, intruders, usurpers of the landscape.

But except for a handful of Costanoans and Miwoks we're all newcomers, intruders, and usurpers. The environment would be in much better shape if we all moved out. But we won't, and neither will the lakes. We won't because there is something happening here, a creative and exciting interchange between the man-made and the natural —— between a misguided technology that builds lakes and a patient nature which clothes these lakes with magic.

Building a lake, for all its ambiguity, has got to be one of the best pieces of magic in the world. It beats anything Houdini has ever done. Take a dry piece of land, add lots of water, wave the magic bulldozer, and stand back. Boom! Reeds, rushes, sedges, willows, tules, and dozens of other water plants burst out of the ground as if they were hiding in ambush, waiting for the day the waters would arrive. Ducks splash down upon the lake and nest in the cattails. Turtles and frogs materialize out of thin air and immediately go about their ancient business. Fish jump out from the depths to snap at water bugs, while the shoreline becomes riddled with the dens of foxes, raccoons, and other animals who prosper near the new lake.

A new lake may look somewhat half-finished for a few years. But after a short time an artificial lake is no longer "artificial" —— at least not to the plants, animals, and birds who inhabit it. Older lakes like Temescal and Chabot which were built 100 years ago have nestled so comfortably into their landscapes that they look as much at home in the East Bay as an oak forest.

The East Bay Regional Park District manages nine lakes. Jewel Lake in Tilden Park is set aside as a bird refuge. The other lakes (Anza, don Castro, Chabot, Contra Loma, Cull Canyon, Shadow Cliffs, Temescal, and del Valle) offer fishing, hiking, boating, and —— except for Chabot —— swimming.

Lake Anza

Lake Anza is a small, nine-acre lake located in Tilden Regional Park. It offers swimming —— and with its cattails, rocky outcroppings, nearby forests, and mountainous landscape it is one of the most picturesque lakes in the Bay Area. I know it, now you know it, but unfortunately we're not alone. Hundreds of thousands of other people know about Lake Anza. And they all seem to show up on hot weekends when you are likely to find *No Admittance, Beach Full* signs posted at the entrance. So be forewarned.

Fishing is also permitted here, but apparently no one has yet told the fish (if there happen to be any).

The lake was built in 1939 by damming up a portion of Wildcat Creek. Its original purpose was to provide water for the lawns and greens of the new Tilden golf course. It was named after Captain Juan Bautista de Anza, the great colonizer of the Southwest, who along with Jose Joaquin Moraga led a brief expedition to this area in 1776.

Lake Anza is one of the best of the Park District's walk-around lakes. The entire hike takes only twenty minutes or so, but it leads you through some truly fine scenery and involves you in several minor adventures: treading across the dam, mountain goating on top of some rocks, crossing Wildcat Creek, and mucking your way through a willow swamp. And there are many side excursions you can take. You can sit out on the rocks that protrude into the lake, posing perhaps like that winged sylph in the old White Rock ads. You can wander out over the meadows. Or you can follow the rushing waters of Wildcat Creek through a dark, rocky canyon of oak, bay, and a few redwoods.

Or if your body seems to be mated to your beach blanket for the day, why not send your head on an exciting journey of its own? The sandy beach and grassy lawns are arranged like an amphitheater where every one looks out across the lake at the spacious scenery of Tilden. If you sit back far enough on the lawn you can also look out over some righteously spacious people —— Berkeleyites who crowd the shores of the lake on hot days. Or for still another great view between swims (I'm serious about this) look straight up and get re-acquainted with the spots before your eyes as they float across the blue sky —— your own, very private, ultimately familiar constellations.

I've enjoyed myself at Lake Anza whenever I've gone, but my favorite times are in the early spring and late fall. The swimming lakes around the Park District are officially closed (except for Del Valle), but if it's a warm day and a life guard is available the Park District will sometimes open Lake Anza for swimming. (Call 531-9300 to find out for sure.) On days like this, when the weather is balmy, the surrounding hills are still green, and there are only a scattering of people on the beach, Lake Anza (which is beautiful in any case) seems to achieve a pastoral perfection.

For further adventures in Tilden, and for a map of Lake Anza, see pages 45-49.

don Castro

Don Castro is not that famous playboy ambassador from Costa Rica. Nor is he the Latin lover who stole grandma's heart way back in the silent picture days. Nor is don Castro the name of a Caribbean revolutionary, a Havana cigar, or a Puerto Rican rum. Even more exotic than these (the truth is indeed stranger than fiction!), don Castro is an artificial lake in Castro Valley. A lake that has fish, turtles, ducks, and frogs as well as a separate swimming area with a clean beach, green lawns, and picnic tables. It was named after Guillermo Castro, a Spanish settler whose immense 27,000 acre land grant included what is now Hayward and Castro Valley.

Don Castro Lake was created in 1964 when the Alameda County Flood Control and Water Conservation District put a dam on the San Lorenzo Creek. The water backed up behind the dam, and within a few years cattails, ducks, fish, and fishermen arrived to complete the lake environment.

In building the dam engineers needed thousands of tons of earth. They got it by flattening a nearby hill, and in the middle of the flat spot they dug a crater. When the lake had formed they pumped water from the lake into the crater and thus created a separate pool —— the "swimming lagoon" as it's called. White sand was poured around the swimming areas, a three and a half acre lawn was planted, and picnic tables, barbecue pits, a bath house, and shade trees were installed. In 1969 don Castro was opened to swimming and picnicking.

The engineering history of don Castro explains why there are two distinct environments here: a fairly natural lake environment for fishermen, hikers, and bird-watchers; plus a developed, carefully planned recreation area for swimmers, picnickers, and sunbathers.

The swimming area is very pleasant and open. It has a roped-off space for little kids so they don't get in your way very much —— and you don't get in theirs. I especially enjoy swimming here on weekends when there is hardly any truck noise on the nearby freeway.

The area around don Castro has been a favorite recreation spot for many hundreds of years. Near where the dam now stands Indians used to have a sweathouse where they'd pass the time of day taking saunas. Later, Chinese gamblers took over the spot and opened up a casino featuring fan-tan, faro, and the other slick gambling games of the last century. Today the East Bay Regional Park District offers swimming, hiking, and fishing. From Indians to Chinese gamblers to us, recreation has gone through some bizarre changes. I sometimes wonder what the next century will bring to don Castro. More inconceivable changes? Or have our culture and our tastes settled into a groove for a dynasty or two?

While most people come to don Castro primarily to swim, I can never resist taking a hike around the lake. I suppose if I put blinders on my eyes I could make the trip in about thirty minutes. It usually takes me at least two hours. There's so much to see, hear, and think about.

You can begin your hike in the eucalyptus grove across from the beach. These trees were obviously planted by people (note the straight rows), and their trunks show signs of a recent fire. The fire brought about a significant change: it burned away the thick duff you usually find under eucalyptus trees and it encouraged a lot of interesting plants to spring up.

As you walk along the edge of the lake, there are many things to be aware of: dragonflies putting on shows of precision darts and dashes, turtles sunning themselves on half-submerged logs, frogs practicing their ventriloquist acts, and the nostalgic hummings and buzzings of a summer afternoon. To make a complete circuit of the lake, follow the shore until the lake narrows into the San Lorenzo Creek. Then take  off your shoes, roll up your cuffs, and wade across the shallow water.

There is nothing really dramatic here, nothing very exciting. Just the scruffy, varied goings-on of a typical piece of left-alone California land. The most intensely moving thing I ever saw here was the battle —— not between a mountain lion and a deer —— but between a garter snake and a mouse. The snake had

74

chomped down on the mouse but was having trouble swallowing it. The mouse was too fat, the snake a mere adolescent. The snake tried and tried, maneuvering the mouse's body around until its head was aimed right down the snake's throat. At that point the squeaking and wiggling stopped. The mouse went limp, resigned to its fate, apparently dead. The snake paused and resumed its struggle, stretching its jaws to outlandish sizes trying to encompass the mouse's body. I watched fascinated. There was something horrible yet vaguely comic about this struggle. The snake rested and tried again. It kept at it for about a half hour. But the mouse was simply too fat. The snake finally gave up, backed off very quickly, and slithered away like a disappointed suitor without even a backward glance. A few seconds later the dead mouse stirred itself, staggered to its feet, wiggled its nose timidly, and ran off into the bushes as if nothing out of the ordinary had happened.

And indeed the mouse was right: nothing out of the ordinary had happened!

If your love of nature is not satisfied by anything less than grandeur —— well, a walk around don Castro will seem a bit silly to you. But if you want to look in on the lives of snakes, mice, dragonflies, hummingbirds, frogs, turtles, ducks, and whatever else you may see; if you have the patience to watch these ordinary animals go about their daily affairs, and if you have the humility to think deeply about their lives; then the walk around don Castro is one of the best short hikes I know. Other grander hikes leave me with the feeling of having been some place special. The walk around don Castro leaves me with the feeling of wanting to return again and again.

Lake Chabot

Lake Chabot is a very peaceful lake. It is big (315 acres) and it feels big; yet because of an island in the middle and its many bays and inlets it seems at the same time intimate. People come to fish, hike, boat, or just sit quietly along the banks. The peacefulness of Lake Chabot is contagious. The only squabbling you are likely to hear is among the ducks and the geese.

Lake Chabot's profound calm gives almost no hint of its grotesque beginnings. The lake was built in 1874 by Anthony Chabot, a hydraulic engineer fresh from the gold country. His method of construction was revolutionary. He first aimed gigantic water hoses at nearby hills and washed thousands of tons of earth into San Leandro Creek. Then he imported herds of wild mustangs to gallop back and forth over the loose earth to compact it into a dam.

The water backed up slowly behind the dam, and by 1876 Lake Chabot was formed. Then nature took over. It revegetated the barren hills and lined the lakeshore with tules. Ducks, herons, and egrets came to nest. Grebes, loons, geese, and coots visited and stayed. Deer broke trails to the shore. Raccoons and foxes found dens along the banks. Man created Lake Chabot, and nature accepted the creation.

But as far as people were concerned, Lake Chabot was a hidden garden. It remained off limits to the public for the next ninety years. Fishermen stared longingly over the fence. Rumors spread about five pound trout and nine pound bass, innocent, reckless fish prowling the lake, ready to chomp down on the first hook.

Even Water Company officials acknowledged that the major "fishing problem" at Lake Chabot was too many fish. This was especially true in the drought of 1918 when the water level dropped drastically. Fish moving through the shallow water stirred up silt which clogged the filters and stopped the flow of water into Oakland. That year imaginative Water Company personnel introduced sea lions into the lake, figuring that the sea lions would eat the fish. But the sea lions had other ideas. Homesick for the salt water, they were seen humping and thumping their way over the hills toward the Bay.

As the years passed the demand for public access to Lake Chabot grew stronger, and in 1966 the Water Company gave in. The fence came down. On opening weekend an estimated 30,000 fishermen stampeded to the lake. And, wonder of wonders, those crazy rumors proved true. Some lucky folks actually did catch five pound trout and nine pound bass. And they still do! Today Lake Chabot is one of the best stocked of all the Park District's lakes, and it is one of the most popular fishing spots in the Bay Area.

The swimming is undoubtedly as good as the fishing, but only the ducks know for sure. Lake Chabot is officially classified as an emergency water supply. And (as you may remember from childhood trespasses) the Law is unbelievably up-tight about people peeing in the water supply. Thus swimming is absolutely forbidden, and many parts of the shoreline are off limits to hikers merely because of the lack of proper toilets. These laws, I'm sorry to report, are strictly enforced by park personnel.

Although you can't swim here, the lake is ideal for boating. It is big enough to make boating an adventure, while its narrow fingers keep you in close contact with the surrounding landscape. You can rent a rowboat, pedal boat, canoe, or an electric motorboat. You can also try the excursion boat which (when it's operating) circles the lake daily throughout the summer and on weekends during the winter. (For schedules and boat rental fees, call 582-2422.)

In addition to boating and fishing, I hope you'll also take a walk. One of my favorite hikes is along the eastern shore of the lake toward Honker Bay. The path is asphalted most of the way, which makes it very good for bikes, baby carriages, and trikes. The further you get from the Marina, the more quiet and pleasant the lake becomes. The vegetation is more varied, with especially fine stands of creambush, cow parsnip, and that pungent smelling plant called mugwort from which absinthe was once made. You pass through some oak-bay woodland, scrub brush, and small meadows —— while along the lake redwinged blackbirds, wavering like flags on cattail stalks, lecture you on the innumerable virtues of being a redwinged blackbird.

Once you enter the narrower parts of Honker Bay you can get to the other side by crossing a footbridge. There is no toll collector here, no customs officials, no change of currency, but beware! You are entering a new country. From the land of shade and coolness you cross over to the land of sunshine and heat. You've passed from a north-facing slope to an exposed south-facing (sun-facing) slope. The temperature is noticeably hotter here, and lizards scurry along the dusty trails, apparently turned on by the heat. Instead of trees and shrubs with broad soft leaves, you find a grassy hillside splotched with stiff coyote brush, and topped by a forest of wispy eucalyptus.

At this point you can walk a bit further around the lake, until you reach the trail that climbs the slope to Las Cumbres Family Campground (see page 99). Or, you can recross the footbridge and follow the fire road away from the lake into some very attractive woods.

Whatever reason you come to Lake Chabot, whether for fishing, hiking, boating, or sightseeing, I think you'll leave feeling very relaxed. There's something about this big body of water that mellows people out. I sometimes imagine that there's a box at the Lake Chabot parking lot labeled, *Abandon all cares, ye who enter.* Every week thousands of people drive into the parking lot and deposit all their cares and worries in this imaginary box. They then walk down to the lake with a buoyant sense of newness and adventure. They paddle a boat over placid waters, try to catch a big fish, hike up fern and oak canyons, lie down to rest in flowery meadows. In the late afternoon they leave, and many of them forget to go back to the box to pick up their cares and worries. Millions of cares and worries get left behind at Lake Chabot, but the box is always empty —— as if the cares and worries were insubstantial to begin with.

To many thousands of visitors, fishing, boating, and hiking at Lake Chabot is a permanent part of the East Bay life. But artificial lakes are never *permanent,* and although there are no obvious signs of it, Lake Chabot is scheduled for a crisis. The dam is now a century old, and it no longer meets the State earthquake code. A whole army of Dutch boys putting their fingers in the dam won't help, either. A big sum of money, running into the millions, must be spent to rebuild the dam. The Water Company (which still owns the lake) feels that spending so much money in this case is economically unjustifiable. But the alternative, draining the water and leaving behind a 315 acre bowl of mud, is totally unthinkable, (especially to the East Bay Regional Park District which manages the lake for recreation). The crisis will soon come to a head, and to date no one knows how it will be resolved. My own hope (and it's merely a hope) is that the State or Federal Government will step in with the money to rebuild the dam and in the process redesignate Lake Chabot as a recreational lake —— complete with fishing, boating, hiking, and —— ah, at last! —— swimming.

(For a map of Lake Chabot, see page 17.)

Contra Loma

Contra Loma is a small lake with a sandy beach, green lawns, and a cattail fringe. It is surrounded by 1,000 acres of grassland. Seen from the air during the summer it looks like a sparkling blue-green jewel set in the vast golden meadows outside Antioch. There's swimming, fishing, and a unique hiking experience.

The first time I visited Contra Loma I tramped around the lake searching for the creek that feeds into it. It was a charming walk. Mallards, canvas backs, coots, and a heron had staked out various parts of the lake. A delegation of Canadian geese followed after me, strutting around like a group of congressmen and bankers. My footsteps triggered off the splashing of frogs, while within the water scores of muskrats were diving, swimming, twisting, playing, disappearing, and reappearing, obviously having a wonderful time. Yet as I checked out the dam and the topography around the lake I didn't find any sizable creek that might have created this lake. There is no big creek, no stream, and (as one might deduce from the dry, nearly treeless hills) there's not much rain here either. It was all very perplexing: where could this water have come from, I wondered. And then I met a fisherman.

"Catch anything?" I asked, and he showed me (believe it or not) a flounder!

So now I had two mysteries: where did the water come from, and what in the world was an ocean fish doing flopping around in this freshwater lake?

Contra Loma (as I later found out) was built in the late 1960's by the U. S. Bureau of Reclamation as a storage reservoir for the Contra Costa Canal System. The water for this system is pumped out of the San Joaquin River at Rock Slough, and it is carried by a network of aqueducts throughout eastern Contra Costa County. The water is used for industrial, agricultural, and in some cases domestic services. At one point pumps draw the water out of the canals and force it up through underground pipes into Contra Loma Lake. (You can see the pumphouse just below the dam.) Here the water sits, waiting patiently in the bullpen, so to speak. If at any time the pumps at Rock Slough have to be shut down for repairs, water will be drawn from Contra Loma to keep the canals operating.

Now that we know where the water comes from we can (my dear Watson) solve the mystery of the misplaced flounder. Flounders are, of course, found in salt water, and they are plentiful in the Bay. From the Bay they have made their way into the Delta and up the San Joaquin River where flounder fry (small enough to pass through the screens) get drawn through the pumps and are dashed and tumbled into the canal system. They swim along the canals until eventually a few get sucked in by a second pump and are deposited in Contra Loma Lake.

Once the flounder fry reach Contra Loma they undergo another, far more astounding journey —— a journey that every member of the flounder family must go through. In their infancy flounder fry are almost indistinguishable from any other small fish. They are symmetrically shaped, a bit like a torpedo, with no hint whatsoever of their future appearance. They hatch from eggs that float upon the surface, and for their first month or so they stay near the surface, feeding on minute organisms. But at the ripe old age of about four weeks, when they are no more than a half-inch long, they desert the surface, sink to the bottom, and lie down on their sides. Then begins a remarkable transformation. The skull twists and distorts until the lower eye (which is staring unproductively at the mud) "migrates" around the top of the head to the up-facing side of the fish. The body flattens out, the lower (eyeless) side turns white, the upper side turns a darker color, and the fins undergo further changes until (how incredible it must be to experience this!) a flounder is created.

"That's an amazing fish you caught," I said to the fisherman.

"Not any more amazing than anything else in the world," he said, and I thought about that for quite a while afterwards.

In addition to flounders and striped bass (another salt water immigrant), Contra Loma also has plentiful trout, black bass, and other freshwater fish.

Many of the people who visit Contra Loma are fishermen, but during the summer most visitors are here to swim. The lake sits in a bowl which collects heat and keeps out the brunt of the wind. On marginal beach days, when it seems a bit chilly in Oakland, you might remember that it's probably just right at Contra Loma.

The land surrounding Contra Loma is predominantly meadowland, nearly 1,000 acres of grass with only a couple of dozen buckeyes and blue oaks scattered over the slopes. During the last century grizzly bears, mountain lions, antelopes, and elk roamed these hills. Captain Kimball, a pioneer resident of nearby Antioch, noted that on the morning of his arrival in 1849 he saw eighty elk in one herd. And much of the meat sold in local markets in 1850-51 was dried elk meat.

Today, of course, the big game is gone, and the land seems much emptier without them. The engineers and park planners who recently arrived to build Contra Loma Lake looked over the undulating golden-brown grasslands and they saw —— well, to be blunt, they saw nothing! Their early reports kept referring to "barren grasslands," and the problem the planners faced was how to make these "barren grasslands" attractive to potential park users. "Plant trees," came the answer. Over 5,000 trees were planted in 1969: Monterey pines, Coulter pines, bishop pines, live oaks, sycamores, white alders, black walnuts, Arizona and Modesto ashes, Fremont poplars, Moraine honey-locusts..... But no sooner were the trees planted than an amazing thing happened. Hordes of rabbits and mice arose out of nowhere and nibbled almost every one of the trees down to the ground. It makes you think. Barren?

To begin with, there are lots of rabbits, mice, moles, gophers, and ground squirrels at Contra Loma. Then there are all the animals that feed off them: gopher snakes, king snakes, rattlesnakes, foxes, badgers, hawks, and vultures. On hot summer days when *you* are most likely to be visiting Contra Loma, the wildlife is most likely to be hiding. But even the briefest walk through the grasslands will turn up dozens of burrows, scats, nibbled grass, and other signs of the rich wildlife that inhabits the grassland.

Despite its proximity to the Bay, Contra Loma is really part of the hot interior grassland environment. In the spring the grass is green and cool, rippling in the wind, flecked with exquisite wildflowers. Everybody loves to hike across the California grasslands in the spring.

But in the heat of summer there is a different sort of experience that is reserved only for the most courageous hikers. Climb to the top of a ridge and look over the big, billowing hills beyond Contra Loma's "bowl" —— hills strewn randomly over the landscape like so many pillows. The ground beneath your feet seems to be breathing with heat waves. You sweat, and sweat, and sweat, and the sun looms big in your consciousness. Ever wonder why many primitive people worship the sun? Here at the top of the hill is a feeling of fullness, vastness, and spaciousness dominated by the intense, powerful presence of the sun. Contra Loma is an especially good place to get to know the sun. In the winter it is shy and kindly, in the spring gently insistent and nurturing. But during the daily summer holocaust the sun shows all its power. At first it may seem as if the sun is angry. Don't fight it, don't try to hide from it. Lie down in the meadow and submit. Let yourself be as passive as a piece of iron in the hands of a blacksmith. Let the sun beat down on you, pound against you, and melt you down into the smells of the meadow until it seems you no longer exist.

From this encounter with the sun you return feeling purified, cleansed, reborn, and perhaps a bit wobbly. Walk down the hill again and jump into the cool waters of Contra Loma Lake for what will undoubtedly be the most refreshing swim you have ever had anywhere.

Cull Canyon

Cull Canyon in Castro Valley is a small park of about 100 acres with a lake. The main attraction here is swimming, although you can also take short hikes into the surrounding meadows, brushlands, and forests.

Like nearby don Castro (page 73), Cull Canyon Lake was the creation of the Alameda County Flood Control and Water Conservation District. Whatever engineering virtues the lake may have, as a swimming hole it is impossible. The water level drops by as much as fifteen feet every year, leaving a broad ribbon of mud all around the shore. To provide for swimming a second dam was built on a side ravine that feeds into the lake. The area behind the dam was graded and landscaped, and water was pumped from the lake to make a small, neat swimming area. Thus there are really two lakes here: the larger lower lake with its ducks, occasional fishermen, and fluctuating water level; and the small upper lake with its tidy beach, bath-house, snack bar, redwood decks, sand, green lawns, and highly landscaped appearance.

While you are at the beach you might notice the pure grassy slopes that rise up behind you. Elsewhere in the area ungrazed meadowland is being encroached upon by brush. But here you won't find a single, solitary piece of brush. Why is this slope different from other slopes in the area? The answer is, *fire*. Every couple of years accidental fires burn off brush seedlings and leave the hillsides blackened for the rest of the summer. When the fall rains come, seeds in the soil germinate and reclothe the slopes with pure stands of oats and a scattering of poppies and vetch. Such meadows are a good environment for deer and other big game. The Indians of California used to ignite their grasslands regularly to burn away the brush and create meadows much like the one above Cull Canyon.

Most people who come to Cull Canyon don't think very much about Cull Creek, the creek that feeds into the lake. In fact they may even be a little contemptuous of it. They know Cull Creek only from what they see near the Bay Tree Picnic Area across Heyer Avenue from the lake —— a small trickle of water dwarfed by a dam, a spillway, and an enormous sculpturesque concrete channel installed by the county Roads Division.

To visit the real, unimproved Cull Creek, go upstream from the park further into Cull Canyon. This is one of the loveliest canyons in the Bay Area. S. W. Cull was a pioneer resident, and I imagine that the canyon is pretty much as he left it. Here and there stands a bulky, rickety, old-fashioned barn or stable, a trim wooden corral fence, and a horse whisking away a fly in the lazy sun. Cull Creek turns out to be a gentle, mellow little creek that flows peacefully between its tree-lined banks. The slopes above the creek are a charming mosaic of cow-dotted meadows and thick oak woodlands stretching widely and leisurely over the hills. If you want to explore this pastoral scene more intimately, go a few miles past the park along Cull Canyon Road to Hideaway Ranch or Big Oak Ranch where you can rent a horse.

The beach at Cull Canyon is a very pleasant place to spend the day swimming and sunbathing —— which is exactly what most people do. But what makes Cull Canyon Park particularly exciting to me is the bird life here. The mixture of meadow, forest, brushland, streamside, and lake provides a varied environment that attracts an incredible number of birds. There are so many birds at Cull Canyon, and they're doing such interesting things, I hope on your next visit you'll check them out.

How do you watch birds? You might, of course, make a big production out of it. You bring binoculars, field guides, boots, a safari hat, a pencil, a notebook, a checklist, decoys, blinds, and a dozen bird whistles. With a look of dour determination on your face you go stomping into the brush and do you know what? At the end of the day you'll be stung, blistered, scratched, tired, and nasty —— and all the birds will have fled into the hills, scared out of their little wits.

Then again, you might be more casual about it. Bird watching can be a lazy man's sport. While you're fishing, sunbathing, or lying under a tree you listen carefully and look. Be quiet, peaceful, alert, and you'll begin to see birds everywhere. You'll see long-legged birds wading on stilts along the stream; web-footed birds paddling across the lake; plump housewifey birds rustling in the leaves; tiny birds buzzing like bees at flowers; hunters and scavengers patrolling the sky; birds with yellow feathers, blue feathers, gold, red, orange, or green feathers; birds gulping insects, stabbing fish, cracking seeds, sipping nectar; birds chasing each other madly through the trees without ever once crashing into the branches. Look around and you'll be amazed at what fantastic things you'll see.

Or forget about looking, close your eyes and listen to the bird songs that fill the air: songs that pierce, twitter, and cascade; songs like bright ribbons spread over the sky; songs tossed down as freely as confetti. I used to imagine that the birds were singing out of joy and sexiness. Now bird scientists tell us that much of the singing is to stake out a territory and warn away intruders. I'm delighted to learn this. What a marvelous way to settle territorial battles. Imagine if every time a person I didn't like came to my door, instead of being rude or grouchy I could chase him away with a song. What songs I would learn to sing! It makes me envy the birds all the more. I envy them their flight, I envy them their ingenious way of settling disputes, and I envy them the privilege of spending each warm summer day around the lake at Cull Canyon.

Shadow Cliffs

Shadow Cliffs is —— well —— to be perfectly honest about it, Shadow Cliffs is a hole in the ground. A 144-acre hole. It lies between Pleasanton and Livermore and has swimming, a sandy beach, excellent fishing, and some boating.

The Sand and Gravel Division of Kaiser Industries began digging the hole in 1930 as a quarry. When they were through digging, they shut off the pumps and the deepest part of the hole filled with water. Now hold onto your seats and dig the economics of this. If *you* were into big business, what would *you* do with a played out, flooded quarry? Obviously you'd try to give it away. In 1969 Kaiser presented this derelict quarry to the East Bay Regional Park District as a "gift." They valued the gift at $250,000 —— thus undoubtedly obtaining some sort of windfall tax write-off. The Park District then used this established land value to get $250,000 in "matching funds" from the U. S. Bureau of Outdoor Recreation, and with the federal money they went to work. They built a sandy beach, lawns, picnic area, and parking lot. They planted some trees and are in the middle of making a playfield. Shadow Cliffs has not yet become the "compact, sparkling recreation area" Park District officials envision. But visit here anyway to groove on the strange, strange, strange feeling of a park growing out of a gravel pit.

Swimming is the most popular activity at Shadow Cliffs, and the water which filters into the lake through the surrounding gravel soil is deliciously clear and cool.

There are also boat rentals and fishing. Black bass, red-eared sunfish, white catfish, Mississippi silverside, and blue-gills have been planted in the lake, while carp have mysteriously sneaked in on their own. The lake is periodically stocked with rainbow trout. What in the world do all these fish find to eat in a place as sterile as an old quarry? Look along the south shore of the lake and you'll see some recently flooded brush and trees protruding from the water. These dead branches are the basis of a lot of the lake's fish life. Algae clings to them, and small forage fish and black bass fry find food and protection among the tangles.

Another place where the fish feed, breed, and hatch is just north of the beach area where you'll notice a grove of bushes extending into the water. These bushes look like willows, but they're not. They go by the provocative name of *mule fat*. Unlike willows, which have long "catkins," these bushes have full, complicated little flowers and puffball seeds that tell you they are members of the Composite family —— close relatives of sunflowers, asters and dandelions. I'm not sure why this plant is called *mule fat*. The best guess I've heard is that mules, which aren't nearly as fussy as horses, browse the bush enthusiastically.

Just over the dikes from Shadow Cliffs is a section of Arroyo del Valle Creek that you might look at. This is a big, broad, green, slow-moving creek lined with willows and alders —— a creek that to my eyes has more exciting and creative recreation than any developed area in the East Bay. And apparently the wildlife feel the same way. You would not ordinarily expect much wildlife in the vicinity of an old gravel pit, but the wildlife around Shadow Cliffs may surprise you. It surprised me. Part of the quarry above the water level has reverted to meadow and brush. I've seen ground squirrels, jack rabbits, raccoons, muskrats, deer, and many birds —— some living here, others (like us) just passing through.

If you are one of those people who never sees wildlife in the wild, let me give you some advice. You're not likely to see many wild animals (aside from *homo sapiens*) at two o'clock on a hot summer Sunday afternoon while sitting on your blanket at a crowded beach. The best time to see wildlife is at odd hours —— dawn, dusk, or cloudy days when there are few other people and no dogs around. Go off into the scrubby meadows, sit down somewhere inconspicuous, and pretend you're a bush. Think like a bush, act like a bush. Be patient, quiet, aware. Pretty soon you'll blend into the other bushes, and you'll be delighted by how much you see.

There's plenty of wildlife, fishing, and swimming at Shadow Cliffs. But beyond that there is something very unique and even bizarre here. All around you at the horizon are the massive towers and conveyer belts of sand and gravel operations. On week days (and sometimes on weekends) you hear the noises of tons of rocks being sorted and poured, of huge equipment scraping and dumping, of boxcars crashing and clanging. It's a monstrous, fascinating, other-worldly scene of big machinery against a sharp blue sky.

The "cliffs" (which are really the sides of the original gravel pit) are eroded, grey, full of shadows, lifeless and bleak.

Lapping up against the cliffs is the water —— cool, clear, peaceful, inviting. Ducks and coots paddle softly about. Fish splash and leave concentric circles. Delicate lacy trees line the water's edge. Everything is cool, clean, sparkling.

On the shore wildflowers are blooming, rabbits scurry in the bushes, and in the tall grass meadow-larks build their nests and raise their brood.

Shadow Cliffs is a combination of exquisite delicacy and mechanical brutality —— as unintegrated, crazy, and surrealistic as the rest of American life. Except more so. Even if you don't swim or fish or care much about wildlife, maybe you ought to drop in on Shadow Cliffs anyway. For the artistic experience.

Temescal

Temescal is a small, very pretty park. It has a lake, green lawns, secluded picnic areas, and a beach with white sand. Weeping willows lean out over the water as if to admire their own reflections. Butterflies flutter across the trimmed grass. Children hold out pieces of bread to white ducks that glide over the lake. Hikers set out on short walks through redwood and pine groves. A few hundred feet away are two brutal freeways and a power station — but these sights and sounds are mostly hidden from Temescal. People stretch out on the beach or on the grass —— some clearly napping, some clearly awake, but most in a dreamlike state somewhere in between.

An amazing thing about Lake Temescal is that most of this charming environment is man-made. The lake, of course, is artificial. The eucalyptus trees in the background come from Australia, the pines that shade the picnic areas are from the Monterey Peninsula, the weeping willows are natives of Eurasia, and even the redwood grove near the south parking lot is man-planted. The big stone building near the beach is the accounting office of the East Bay Regional Park District. Every sunny morning a maintenance man turns on the nearby miniature waterfall, and turns it off again before he goes home. The white ducks are domestic fowl gone wild. Very little is native at Temescal, including us.

But if Temescal is so artificial, why in the world is it so pretty? Who was the genius that created this place? Was it Anthony Chabot who built the lake? Or the East Bay Regional Park District which runs it? Will the talented landscape architect in charge of this project please step forward and take a bow? But no one steps forward. The landscape architect, always present, forever modifying everything we do, is simply *Time*.

Lake Temescal is the oldest lake in the East Bay. It was created in 1868 by Anthony Chabot. He built it the way he later built Lake Chabot, by aiming gigantic water hoses at the surrounding land, washing tons of earth into the creek, and compacting the earth under the hooves of wild horses.

Lake Temescal was originally meant to supply the tiny town of Oakland with water. But we all know what happened to the "tiny town of Oakland," and by the 1870's larger reservoirs had completely replaced Temescal. The lake was left alone to grow old and mellow. Time chipped away at the sharp edges of artificiality, blended the diverse elements that were later added, erased what didn't belong, and shaped Temescal into the most natural-looking and organic of all the artificial lakes.

Before Temescal was a lake it was, of course, a creek. Costanoan Indians had a village along its shores, and in the village they erected a communal sweat house. The sweat house looked like an upside-down bowl and held as many as fifty men. The men lit a roaring fire inside and danced around the fire for hours until, limp with exhaustion, they opened the door and flung themselves into the cool stream. They used the sweat house to cleanse themselves (like a sauna), to cure illness, and perhaps as part of a spiritual exercise. Before going on a hunt they bathed thoroughly to rid their bodies of human odors, and then they rubbed pungent herbs over their bodies to become even more like the vegetation around them. Franciscan missionaries named the creek "Temescal," a name they derived from two Aztec words: *tema* (to bathe), and *cali* (a house).

Today, of course, these primitive Indians are gone. They have been replaced by modern, progressive, civilized *us*. Yet on hot summer days we cover ourselves with odorous oils, lie in the hot sun to develop a sweat, and then —— limp with exhaustion —— fling ourselves into the cool waters of Temescal.

To thousands of Oakland-Berkeley residents summertime means Lake Temescal. It is our backyard swimming pool, and the lake is very popular —— especially on weekends. If you want to enjoy a little solitude, come on weekdays or at "off" hours.

If you don't care about swimming, but you are looking for an exceptionally lovely walk within minutes of the city, try Temescal on a foggy morning, when wisps of fog chase each other like young puppies across the glass-like water, and when the lake with its backdrop of trees looks like a scene from a Chinese landscape painting. Or come during a light drizzle when the rain patters softly on the water, and the whole world seems painted in shades of grey. On such drizzly winter days

your arrival is greeted by a delegation of geese who waddle out of the water ——
fierce-looking, honking geese, dancing heavily toward you like a line of over-
weight cheerleaders, whooping it up for the local river god who still presides over
the happenings at Temescal.

del Valle

Del Valle is a huge 3,500 acre park with a lake five miles long. It is located in the hills above Livermore, and it has swimming, boating, fishing, camping (see page 105), and hiking.

It was along one of the hiking trails here that I once spent the morning watching a bird gather materials for its nest. The bird flew from the brush to a nearby meadow and plucked out a piece of straw. But it did not rush right back to its nesting site. Instead it flew with the straw to the top of a bush. There it paused for a long time, rocking in the wind, balancing itself with the straw like a tight-rope walker with a balancing pole. And it sang a song. The song was a torrent of clear sound, continuing so long and so loud that I was amazed that such a drab bird could possibly contain so much of it. I half expected the bird to collapse like a deflated baloon from its efforts. But at the end of the song the bird looked just as plump and fresh as before. It then hopped to the top of another bush and again surveyed the landscape. Finally, after several more bushes and another aria or two, it plunged into the thickest part of the brush and disappeared. A few minutes later it emerged again to fetch another piece of straw. The whole process was unhurried and leisurely. An efficiency expert would have been appalled at all the unnecessary flourishes and wasted motions. "Now this is the proper way to build a nest," I can hear him lecturing. But when you visit del Valle, listen to the birds within you, not the built-in crew of efficiency experts we all carry around. I hope that you'll spend your day here wastefully and creatively —— with the same unhurried and alert exuberance as a bird building its nest.

Del Valle is one of the best places you can go to quiet a noisy mind or relax a restless body. It is big enough to absorb you easily. In fact the size of the lake and the surrounding land puts del Valle in a category of its own. While most of the other lakes in the East Bay are neighborhood swimming holes, del Valle is more on the scale of a State or National Recreation Area. (In fact officially it is a State Recreation Area, managed by the East Bay Regional Park District.)

The lake has seventeen miles of shoreline, and you can swim anywhere and at any time —— without a lifeguard or a snack bar peering over your shoulder. You can also rent a boat, or bring your own —— a rowboat if you want to exercise your arms, a pedal boat if you want to exercise your legs, a sailboat if you want to exercise your brain outmaneuvering the tricky little winds that (sometimes) come in from the surrounding hills. During the summer this long, narrow, placid lake is busy with the activities of thousands of swimmers, fishermen, and boaters. But in early fall most of this activity abruptly ends, as the lake goes through a drastic change.

To understand this change you have to know something about the way the lake works. It was built in 1968 by the State of California as part of the South Bay Aqueduct and State Water Project. Unlike other lakes in the area where recreation was an afterthought, the primary justification for building del Valle was recreation. Other reasons given were flood control and water conservation. The water that fills the lake comes from Arroyo del Valle Creek, but in dry years the State pumps extra water from the Delta to bring the lake up to recreational standards. And the State keeps the lake brim-full until about September 15. By then the kids have returned to school and recreation demands decline. At the same time the South Bay Counties —— Santa Clara and San Jose —— are experiencing their seasonal water shortages. So the valves are opened, and the waters of del Valle begin a southward journey. During the fall the water level in the lake drops by as much as eight inches a day.

Before the lake was built, there was a magnificent, broad valley here, shaded by immense sycamores, pines, and oaks. And throughout the fall as I watch the water

level drop, I keep hoping that this magnificent valley will reappear, intact and magical, like the lost city of Atlantis. But of course it doesn't. The valley is irretrievably lost, replaced by this serene and stately lake. The immense valley trees no longer shade cattle or hold nests of birds, but they still serve life-sustaining functions. They lie at the bottom of the lake where they provide homes and nutrients for the large fish population of del Valle. These trees, with the help of heavy stocking, make this one of the best fishing lakes in the Bay Area, with its large numbers of trout and black bass. And all winter long, as the lake begins to swell once more from the incoming waters of the creek, del Valle is left primarily to fishermen and to the few hikers who continue to wander over the hills.

The land around del Valle is quite different from any other park land in the East

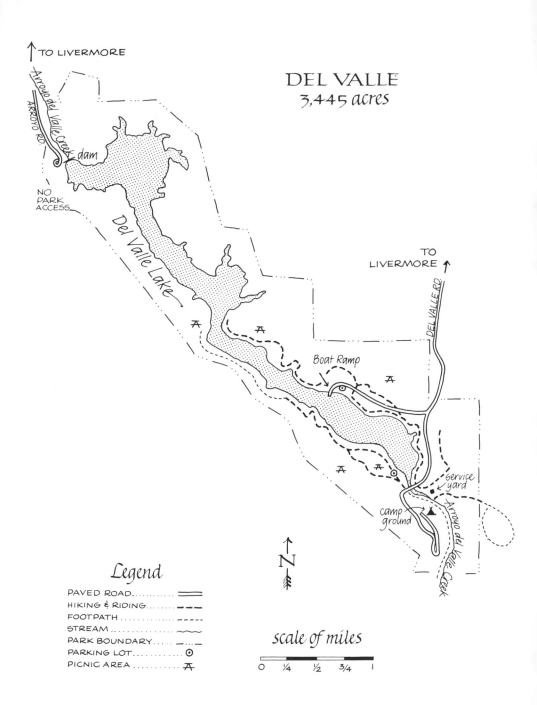

TO LIVERMORE

DEL VALLE
3,445 acres

Arroyo del Valle Creek

ARROYO RD.

dam

NO
PARK
ACCESS

Del Valle Lake

TO
LIVERMORE

DEL VALLE RD

Boat Ramp

service
yard

camp
ground

Arroyo del Valle Creek

Legend

PAVED ROAD............	═══
HIKING & RIDING........	▬ ▬ ▬
FOOTPATH..............	▬ ▬ ▬
STREAM...............	〜
PARK BOUNDARY.....	▬ ‥ ▬
PARKING LOT............	⊙
PICNIC AREA...........	⅄

N

scale of miles

0   ¼   ½   ¾   1

Bay. In other places we are accustomed to the struggle between meadowland and forests. On dry sites the grass wins out, on moist sites we find thick, condensed forests. But at del Valle the battle seems to be a draw. Thriving broad meadows are dotted everywhere by trees. The trees are not close enough together to form a true forest and overshadow the grasses. So grass and trees live together in peaceful co-existence, and the result is perhaps the best of both environments. You can enjoy the shade, character, and bird life of a forest while wandering through open flowery meadows. Yellow-billed magpies strut around like movie stars. Ground squirrels race into their holes at the slightest provocation. Cows with dull, grumpy faces graze among the soft blades of grass. I wonder: has any one ever gotten a cow to smile? At del Valle there is plenty of time for such speculation.

In the winter and spring del Valle has one of the most inviting environments I know, beckoning you to leave the trails and roads and wander aimlessly along the lakeshore, into the cool canyons, and high up into the billowing hills.

During the summer, however, the sun bakes down upon the valley. The hiking season now ends as people gather around the shores of the lake to swim and keep cool.

During the hottest days of summer you might look up at the surrounding hills and wonder how in the world the various plants survive the intense heat. Why don't they just wither and die? Every plant you see at del Valle has had to solve the problem of summer heat, and some of their solutions are ingenious.

Sycamores and willows handle the problem quite simply. They grow near creeks with their roots perpetually in water. As the sun draws moisture out of their flat broad leaves, more moisture is drawn up from the groundwater below.

Plants like the digger pine and chemise have solved the heat problem by reducing their leaves to thin needles. Digger pines have such thin needles, in fact, that these trees have a hazy, cloud-like appearance. The less leaf surface there is, the less water evaporates.

Other plants —— like live oak, coyote bush, and manzanita —— have developed thick leaves coated with a waxy substance, cutin, which protects the inner cells from the intense heat.

The leaves of black sage are covered by a tiny forest of hairs. At night these fuzzy hairs trap moist air next to the leaf's surface, and they maintain this friendly microclimate during most of the next day.

Then there is the buckeye tree which is deciduous. But instead of dropping its leaves during the fall like other deciduous trees, the buckeye loses its leaves during the heat of summer. It conserves water by going completely dormant in the hottest months.

Annual wildflowers handle the summer heat by trustingly dying each spring. Only the seeds lay on the hot earth all summer, closed up tight against the endless beating of the sun. In the fall the first rains come, but the seeds don't respond yet. They are waiting for moisture plus a warming soil, and this combination acts upon them like a trigger. Sometime in February the trigger goes off, and bang! Del Valle is suddenly transformed. Hiking now takes on a new excitement. Throughout the green grass there are explosions and the sparks fly everywhere. Wild fireworks spread over the ground. Flowers pour out over the meadows and flow right down to the borders of the lake. It is during this season that I want to pull every one away from their t.v. sets, kidnap them if necessary, and get them out to del Valle. The ground is covered with lillies, poppies, baby blue-eyes, shooting stars, Chinese houses, paintbrushes —— literally hundreds of different species of wildflowers. Some are soft, open, and utterly passive, like beds of silk sheets. Others are sharply defined, full of secrets and complexity. I love their soft living colors, their textures, and their fragrances. I have even come to love the thick sensuous silence that flowers surround themselves with. But my love is unrequited. It is not for me (or for you) that these flowers put on their annual show, but for the bees who will probe and twist within their silent wombs to complete the act of reproduction. Each flower strains to be as beautiful as it can to capture, seduce, for a few seconds enslave a bee that will complete its cycle. There are spring days at del Valle when I too would willingly be enslaved, but it is our destiny to stand outside this sensuous world that scarcely acknowledges our existence —— to stand outside it like strangers at a wedding, and to wonder at its almost excruciating beauty.

Camping

One day the people of Oakland discovered that some one had stolen night.
The old folks remembered it dimly. Children's books still talked about it along
with elves, kings, queens, trolls, and other bygone things. But no one remembered
having seen a real night for many years.

Some people said it had been stolen by television. Others accused P.G.& E.,
the private automobile, the major oil companies, street lights, and the frantic
pace of 20th century living. At one point it was even rumored that night had
never been stolen at all, but was lurking undiscovered in certain side streets and
alleyways. Some of the braver citizens banded together for mutual protection
and ventured out to verify the rumors. But instead of night all they found were
a few, paltry patches of darkness. Too bad, the old ones muttered: night has
gone the way of the silent movies.

Cheer up, people of Oakland! I bring you good news. You can find plenty of
night —— pure, gorgeous, wholesome, sensuous night —— at three East Bay Regional Park District campgrounds. There's so much night here that you can sleep
in it, sniff it, listen to it, even roll in it. You can watch it creep out from among
the late afternoon shadows, thicken between the hills, and drape itself delicately
around the trees. It pushes nearby rocks and bushes into obscurity, while it draws

the distant stars and moon close in upon us.

With a lantern or campfire you might, of course, hollow out a section of the night. With a flashlight you can punch a tunnel right through it. But when the night is big and healthy it will seal the holes and tunnels again without showing even the slightest scar. Night is not merely lack of day: it has sounds, smells, flowers, wildlife, a spirit, and an existence all its own.

The three campgrounds run by the East Bay Regional Park District are Las Cumbres in the Oakland Hills, del Valle in the Livermore Hills, and Sunol near the town of Sunol. They are all close enough to encourage a spur-of-the-moment camping trip whenever you want to shake up your routine.

For new campers these campgrounds offer the challenge of cooking over a fire (if you can get one going), sleeping on the lumpy ground, and washing burnt pots and pans in icy water. There is also the grateful discovery after your first night camping that you were not eaten by mountain lions, your tent was not trampled by cows, and your toes did not suffer from frostbite. For those of us who have mastered the basic expertise, there is satisfaction in the craftsmanship of camping, a sense of self-sufficiency and ease, and (best of all) a profound feeling of trust that if we give ourselves over to the land it will take good care of us and show us a good time. Which it will, indeed, at these three neighborhood campgrounds.

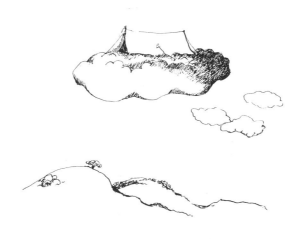

Las Cumbres Campground

Las Cumbres Campground is located twelve miles from downtown Oakland in Anthony Chabot Regional Park (page 14). The Campground cost well over a half-million dollars to build, but don't let that keep you away. The money doesn't show here. In fact Las Cumbres is a very simple, almost Spartan, campground. It has seventy sites arranged in clusters throughout an airy eucalyptus forest on the ridges above Lake Chabot. There's room for twelve trailers. There are flush toilets and (rub-a-dub-dub) hot showers.

The campground is open all year. If there is no attendant at the entrance kiosk, you can pick up the combination to the campground gate at the ranger station, 7901 Redwood Road, a few minutes drive from the campground.

I have had a very personal relationship with Las Cumbres. It brings back such vivid memories that I cannot see it freshly any more, the way you as a casual weekend camper might want it to be presented. When the campground first opened in 1972, I lived there in a tent for nearly three months as a semi-official caretaker. The mere mention of Las Cumbres brings back a flood of associations and memories: my son Reuben (then two years old) clad only in sneakers running through the woods; my wife Rina pushing a wisp of hair out of her face as she hikes up the hill from Lake Chabot; the disdainful fox who lived near the entrance and who told me with a swish of his tail and a haughty over-the-shoulder glance how much he resented my arrival each night; the family of deer who came every evening to taste the delicacies of our newly planted lawns; the silvery glitter of millions of eucalyptus leaves shimmering like scimitars in the breeze; the roost tree behind the telephone booth at the entrance which contained the silent powerful presence of a redtail hawk; our twilight walks down to Lake Chabot which croaked with the voices of a thousand unseen frogs; the time we returned after a two-week vacation to find twenty-eight mice (we counted them!) living in our tent; the period of peacefulness, hope, and joy during the first part of our stay; our sadness as we watched the grass change from green to brown; the sense of isolation that crept in (almost unnoticed) when friends from the city visited us less and less frequently; the lone-liness of Reuben without playmates; and (at last) the knowledge so painfully ar-rived at that camping is great for a month or two, but as a way of life it is not for us.

That was my experience at Las Cumbres. Since, however, there is a fourteen-day limit, there's not much chance that you'll have the same experience I did. You will most likely find that Las Cumbres is a very good place to camp for a short per-iod of time. (It's also a very good place to put up visiting friends and relatives.) It is close to the major East Bay cities. The sites are pleasant, lightly shaded by eucalyptus trees, airy, relatively free of mosquitos and flies, and they offer splen-did panoramic views of the surrounding countryside and Lake Chabot.

There is a lot of peacefulness at Las Cumbres. In fact for some people there is an overdose of peacefulness. If you are looking for a quiet time away from things, Las Cumbres is ideal. You can tie a hammock between two trees, grab a book you've been meaning to read for ages, stretch out on the hammock, spread the book carefully over your belly, and fall asleep. Scenes like this abound at Las Cumbres where the most popular activities of the moment are napping, eating, and taking showers in the hot water shower stalls.

If, however, you want a more active time, you should bear in mind that enter-tainment is not going to jump out from behind the eucalyptus trees and seize you, but that you will have to go out and seek your own entertainment. Here are some ideas on where to go and what to do:

...Hike into the gentle, rolling, generous hills and meadows of Anthony Chabot Regional Park that surround the campground. (*Las Cumbres* in Spanish means "The Hilltops.")

...Explore the eucalyptus environment (see page 28).

...Hike down to Lake Chabot (about one and a half hours round trip) for fish-ing, bird watching, frog watching, or simply watching your own reflections.

...For the kids you might consider bringing a plastic wading pool, badminton rackets, kites, horseshoes, and other appropriate toys.

...If you want to use your car, the following Regional Parks are within fifteen or twenty minutes of Las Cumbres: Cull Canyon, don Castro, Redwood, and Lake Chabot.

...Or if on this camping trip you want to be rid of your car entirely, you can take an A. C. Transit bus (15A) to 11500 Skyline Boulevard (near the corner of Redwood Road), then backpack through Redwood Park along Dunn Trail to West Ridge Trail, south to MacDonald Gate, then through Anthony Chabot Park to Las Cumbres. This hike is about eight to ten miles each way, with a night stay at Las Cumbres. For a shorter hike, you can take the 56A bus to the corner of Golf Links

Road and Grass Valley Road, and from there walk to Chabot Gate and through Anthony Chabot Park to the campground. (For the appropriate maps, see pages 16 and 34.) Frankly, I find it very exciting that we can take a bus to the city outskirts and then hike to a place as peaceful and away-from-it-all as Las Cumbres.

Sunol Campground

Every morning a flock of magpies passes through the Sunol campground to check out the garbage cans. The magpies have yellow beaks, stunning black and white coats, and long irridescent tails. Their elegance is almost embarrassing. It's like having members of the Metropolitan Opera orchestra in full dress searching through your left-overs.

Except for the formality of the magpies, however, Sunol campground is a casual, unpretentious place. There are only about a dozen official camp sites. (An official campsite is one with a picnic table, barbecue pit, and tent pad.) They are clustered together in an oak-bay forest on the banks of Alameda Creek. Above them (and out of sight) is a parking lot where trailers, pickup campers, and V. W. busses huddle together like covered wagons.

Sunol campground is often used as a launching pad for other activities. The hills around it provide some of the most exciting hiking in the Bay Area (see page 39). For athletic ten-speeders the campground is a good starting point for bike trips to the historic towns of Sunol, Niles, and Mission San Jose. But for most people Sunol campground is a place where you can lie back, toast a few marshmallows, and get acquainted with a fascinating forest and a noble creek.

At first glance the forest here is mostly oaks, bay trees, and a few streamside sycamores. But walk through the campground looking at the forest floor and you'll discover that almost all the young trees are bays. The evidence is very dramatic. In the not too distant future this forest will very probably become a pure bay forest.

This is not a very unusual phenomenon, and some foresters feel that the East Bay is entering the "Age of the Bay Tree." In many other hardwood forests —— especially where there is cattle-grazing, heavy deer-browsing, or widespread people-trampling —— you might notice an unexpectedly large percentage of bay saplings among the new growth.

They survive and reproduce fairly well on disturbed soil, and cattle and deer will eat almost anything else before they taste the strongly aromatic leaves of the bay tree. Forests change slowly, of course, and it will be a hundred years or more before we can be certain of this trend, but it seems likely that the bay tree is becoming the dominant tree of the East Bay.

But while forests change slowly, Alameda Creek has undergone some very rapid transformations. The first Spanish explorers found the creek lined with sycamores and willows, looking very much like an arcade —— or *alameda* in Spanish. This full, always-flowing creek so impressed itself upon the early settlers that they eventually named the county of Alameda after it.

But in recent years Alameda Creek has been shamefully degraded. Upstream, the San Francisco Water Department has built a dam to divert the water through a tunnel and into the Calaveras Reservoir. Downstream sections of the creek have been sentenced to life imprisonment within the stone and concrete channels of the Army Corps of Engineers. But at Sunol the creek is still pure and wild —— and for those who know it well it is one of the most nourishing features of Alameda County.

In the spring the creek is thirty or forty feet wide and waist deep. It flows with steadiness, power, and determination not found in any other East Bay creek. Walk along its shores. A few hundred yards past the campground the land spreads out into a broad valley where tall oaks and sycamores shade Sunol's main picnic areas, and where flowery meadows flow down to the banks of the creek. You lie back in the cool, green, springtime grass and watch as the creek catches the sun, dashes it to pieces, strains it out over the riffles, restores it whole in a quiet pool, and tosses it back at you with an unexpected glint.

About a mile past these green-grass, sunlit meadows along a pastoral country lane the valley turns into a steep canyon called "Little Yosemite." Here jumbles of rock and boulders break up the steady flow of the stream. The water rushes through this dark, steep gorge, dashing against the rocks, splitting into hundreds of little waterfalls, and settling down to rest in dozens of calm pools. For those who can jump from rock to rock across the stream, Little Yosemite is an especially primitive and wild place.

During the summer the stream's flow diminishes. If (like most people) you limit your wildlife experiences to birds, deer, squirrels, and rabbits you might want to roll up your pants and wade out into the exotic environment of Alameda Creek. Among the creatures you will find are: waterstriders who perform the daily miracle of walking on water and whose shadows seem more real than their bodies; water scorpions; water boatsmen who row rapidly with their "oars;" turtles;

frogs; whirligig beetles; the larvae of many familiar insects; and several kinds of fish, worms, and plants. This creek has prey, predators, and scavengers who make up a complete wildlife community —— a community that is probably less explored than the wildlife of the remotest parts of Africa.

For a different awareness of Alameda Creek you might try walking along its banks at night. Alameda Creek (like all streams) is blind, and at night one feels very close to it. Its night song is powerful, filling the air. And above the creek rise the jagged branches of trees like bolts of black lightning against a starry sky.

At night you return to the campground and fall asleep listening to the deep, throaty murmurings of the creek. The river sounds flow through your mind and cleanse your consciousness. You awake in the morning to a cool dawn, a sparkling creek, and a flock of magpies. You awake onto a world that is fresh and newborn, a world of which you feel very much a part.

del Valle Campground

Del Valle is one of the few campgrounds where you can stick your head out of the sleeping bag and stare into the face of a cow. When you camp at del Valle you don't seem to be interrupting things very much by your presence. Even on hot weekends —— when all fifty sites are full and trailers come floating through like luxury liners looking for a berth —— del Valle seems to absorb its human visitors as unconsciously as it absorbs its cattle and its varied wildlife.*

The campground is within walking distance of the lake (see page 92). But it is hidden away in a broad flat valley. This valley is the handiwork of the Arroyo del Valle Creek, one of the major tributaries of Alameda Creek. Arroyo del Valle is not one of those ambitious, upstart little mountain creeks that rushes along, eager to make its mark in the world by carving a deep, steep canyon. It finished its carving and gouging many thousands of years ago. Now it has slowed down to enjoy a leisurely old age, as it meanders gently through the serene valley it created in its wilder youth.

This is a fairly old valley, full of towering trees. Standing alongside the creek are the sycamores —— chunky and twisted as trolls —— with their frivolous pompom seeds. Massive oaks spread out, expansive, like monarchs at a feast. The digger pines are eccentric —— literally. They defy gravity, straining off to one side as if reaching for something beyond their grasp.

In the branches blue jays hop and squawk at the earth-bound campers below them. Raccoons and feral housecats plot burglaries on garbage cans. But the acorn woodpeckers scarcely acknowledge the tents and trailers as they carry on their utterly remarkable lives.

Acorn woodpeckers are handsome, swashbuckling birds with black and white flecked bodies and red caps. They live in colonies (actually communes) of about six to fifteen birds. If you look among the sycamores in early May you'll notice the youngsters crawling out of the nest. They are at first wide-eyed, over-eager, and a bit clumsy, and they are always under the watchful eye of an adult. Any adult will do, since the whole colony shares equally in incubating the eggs, feed-

*In 1974 the campground was enlarged and improved. It is hoped that it will absorb the "improvements" easily.

ing and caring for the young, collecting food, and defending the territory.

The diet of the acorn woodpeckers is more varied than their name implies. You might see them feeding off the sap that exudes from tiny holes they have drilled into certain trees. In the spring and summer you'll see them perched on high branches from which they take long "hawking" flights after flying insects. But their most remarkable trait is the way they store a-corns. They store food on a scale unequalled by any other bird. Their warehouses, or storage trees, are found throughout the campground, old giants of trees riddled with thousands of holes. Every year the woodpecker colony adds only 200 or 300 new holes. So these old trees are like heirlooms, handed down and improved upon by many generations of this particular woodpecker co-lony.

Throughout the fall they work noisily and efficiently fitting acorns into the holes. The fit must be tight, as you are well aware if you try to remove an acorn. But the acorns tend to dry and shrink within their holes. The woodpeckers now scramble over the storage trees and re-arrange their riches into smaller holes, like shopkeepers taking inventory of their stock. The same acorn may be moved as many as three times before it is finally eaten.

By mid-winter the crop is safely stored, and the colony can relax a little. At this time of year soft muffled hammerings fill the campground as the colony pecks out a few more holes to use next year and to pass along to future generations of woodpeckers.

For the kids, as well as for the woodpeckers, del Valle is a hospitable environment. There are good climbing trees and other kids to play with, while the two loop roads in the campground see a heavy traffic of bikes, trikes, and a variety of pushem-pullem toys.

But the biggest attraction of all is the creek. Arroyo del Valle flows wide and full until mid-summer. Every spring the Park District pushes some gravel around to create a temporary dam and form a big pool for the bigger kids. Further up-stream are several natural pools —— middle-sized pools for the middle-sized kids, smaller pools for the smaller kids, and little pee-warm pools for the very littlest kids. Even for adults there is no better way of spending a hot, fly-buzzy summer day than to sit among the rounded river rocks, splash in the pools, and look after butterflies and dragonflies as they flick and flutter among the creek willows, nes-tled and sheltered within the valley walls.

At night the gentle hammerings of the woodpeckers and the shouts of the kids are replaced by the hoots of owls, the piping of bats, and the chirps of insects. The gravelly voice of the creek seems louder now. I usually sleep in the open so I can listen to these night songs and engage in one of the oldest pursuits of our species —— stargazing.

Even modern science has not stolen away the wonderment we feel toward the stars. If anything it has added to it. Modern telescopes, for example, have examined the bowl of the big dipper and discovered —— no, not milk as in the old tale, but something more astonishing. In this one tiny area, black and empty to the naked eye, they have found literally millions of stars. In fact they have found whole galaxies, over 1,500 of them. Looking up at the stars, mulling over the inconceivable concept of light years, the meaning of infinity, and the possibilities presented by other galaxies, stretching the mind out over the whole expanse of the sky —— this is the best way I know of sharpening our awareness of our basic condition: that we are tiny beings on the skin of an insignificant planet hurtling through the vast, empty womb of the universe.

Appendix

I shudder to think what the East Bay would be like if it were not for the East Bay Regional Park District. Homes, roads, and telephone poles would have spread from the cities out over the hills. Tilden, Redwood, Sunol, and most of our finest parkland would probably be covered by vast fields of ticky-tacky. Lakes like Chabot, don Castro, and Contra Loma might still be fenced off, and virtually all public swimming would take place in tiled urban pools with their chain-link environments and chlorine smells. Any one wanting to get away from it all would have to undertake a long, exasperating drive to the State and National Parks outside our area. Without the East Bay Regional Park District we would live in a more crowded, frantic, ugly, vastly impoverished area —— if we cared to live here at all.

As early as the 19th century a few visionaries (like Frederick Law Olmstead, architect of New York's Central Park) had suggested that the Oakland-Berkeley Hills be set aside as a natural area. But in those days the whole East Bay was by and large a "natural area" of wooded canyons and rolling pastures, and no one felt the need to put aside any land.

The impetus to create a park district came in the 1920's when the East Bay Municipal Utilities District (EBMUD) was formed to build a pipeline from the Sierras and consolidate the operations of several small independent water companies that were then serving the East Bay. As part of its "dowry" EBMUD received 40,000 acres of watershed land in the East Bay Hills. It felt, however, that it needed only 30,000 acres, and the remaining 10,000 acres (including what is now Tilden, Roundtop, and Redwood Regional Parks) were declared surplus and up for sale. The automobile had made this rugged back-country accessible, and conservationists —— afraid that the lands would be lost to developers —— caused the formation of a special governmental district, the East Bay Regional Park District, to buy these surplus lands and manage them as parks. The first purchases took place in the mid-1930's. The Park District lawyer who negotiated them was Earl Warren, later governor of California and Chief Justice of the U. S. Supreme Court.

Since then the Park District has grown to include over 29,000 acres of

land distributed among nearly two dozen parks. The citizens within its bound-
aries (most of Contra Costa and Alameda counties) support the Park District
by paying an assessment on their property tax. The rate in 1974 is 20¢ per $100
evaluation. As this works out, if you live in a house valued at $20,000, you
pay $10 a year toward the East Bay Regional Park District. Most of this money
is used for land acquisition, a smaller part for maintenance and development.

The East Bay Regional Park District is now nearly 40 years old, and it has
been of tremendous benefit to the people, plants, and wildlife of the East Bay.
We can hardly'do without it. But like any other middle-aged public bureaucracy,
the East Bay Regional Park District desperately needs public involvement. At
stake are such issues as whether future land acquisitions should include more
recreation areas, more pocket picnic areas, more city-oriented parks, or more
semi-wilderness areas. What kind of development should be encouraged? Should
there be more horse trails or more hiking trails? More public campgrounds? More
concession stands? These are some of the questions that are constantly being
debated, often with hardly any public input. The management and staff are
"public servants", but in truth they are seldom approached by the public they
theoretically serve. The Board meetings are open to all, but hardly any one
attends. Hundreds of thousands of people visit the parks each year, but only
a handful ever write or telephone to express their opinions. Within the last
four years you helped elect a member of the Board of Directors: do you re-
member whom you voted for, or what your candidate stood for, or what his
voting record has been since he was elected? As long as we all think that things
will take care of themselves, the Park District is bound to rest on its past
accomplishments, become less and less responsive to our needs, and ultimately
decay.

We all need a strong, sensitive, visionary East Bay Regional Park District.
And the only way to make it strong, sensitive, and visionary is to feed it as
much criticism, praise, energy, and involvement as each of us can afford.

The offices of the East Bay Regional Park District
are at 11500 Skyline Boulevard, Oakland, Ca. 94602.
The telephone number is 531-9300 for information
on Board meetings, or anything else you need to know.

This book is published by
Heyday Books
Box 9145
Berkeley, Ca. 94709

Additional copies or gift copies
may be ordered. Please add 35¢
a book to cover sales tax, postage,
and handling.